EVENTS THAT CHANGED THE WORLD

1960–1980

The Twentieth Century

EVENTS THAT
CHANGED THE
WORLD

1960–1980

=== The Twentieth Century ===

**Other books in the
Events That Changed the World series:**

1900–1920
1920–1940
1940–1960
1980–2000

EVENTS THAT CHANGED THE WORLD

1960–1980

=== The Twentieth Century ===

Jennifer A. Bussey, *Book Editor*

Daniel Leone, *President*
Bonnie Szumski, *Publisher*
Scott Barbour, *Managing Editor*

GREENHAVEN
PRESS ®

THOMSON
—————★—————™
GALE

San Diego • Detroit • New York • San Francisco • Cleveland
New Haven, Conn. • Waterville, Maine • London • Munich

© 2004 by Greenhaven Press. Greenhaven Press is an imprint of The Gale Group, Inc.,
a division of Thomson Learning, Inc.

Greenhaven® and Thomson Learning™ are trademarks used herein under license.

For more information, contact
Greenhaven Press
27500 Drake Rd.
Farmington Hills, MI 48331-3535
Or you can visit our Internet site at http://www.gale.com

LIBRARY OF CONGRESS CATALOGING-IN-PUBLICATION DATA

1960–1980 / Jennifer A. Bussey, book editor.
    p. cm. — (Events that changed the world)
    Includes bibliographical references and index.
    ISBN 0-7377-1758-0 (lib. bdg. : alk. paper) —
    ISBN 0-7377-1759-9 (pbk. : alk. paper)
        1. World Politics—1955–1965—Sources. 2. World politics—1965–1975—
    Sources. 3. World Politics—1975–1985—Sources. 4. Cold War—Sources. I. Bussey,
    Jennifer A. II. Series.
    D848.A18 2004
    909.82'6—dc21   2003053929

Printed in the United States of America

CONTENTS

Beyond its tangible benefits, it had profound symbolic significance in the world arena.

Event 9: *Roe v. Wade* Legalizes Abortion in All Fifty States: January 22, 1973

Event 10: President Richard Nixon Resigns: August 8, 1974

In 1543 a Polish astronomer named Nicolaus Copernicus published a book entitled *De revolutionibus orbium coelestium* in which he theorized that Earth revolved around the Sun. In 1688, during the Glorious Revolution, Dutch prince William of Orange invaded England and overthrew King James II. In 1922 Irish author James Joyce's novel *Ulysses*, which describes one day in Dublin, was published.

Although these events are seemingly unrelated, occurring in different nations and in different centuries, they all share the distinction of having changed the world. Although Copernicus's book had a relatively minor impact at the time of its publication, it eventually had a momentous influence. The Copernican system provided a foundation on which future scientists could develop an accurate understanding of the solar system. Perhaps more importantly, it required humanity to contemplate the possibility that Earth, far from occupying a special place at the center of creation, was merely one planet in a vast universe. In doing so, it forced a reevaluation of the Christian cosmology that had served as the foundation of Western culture. As professor Thomas S. Kuhn writes, "The drama of Christian life and the morality that had been made dependent upon it would not readily adapt to a universe in which the earth was just one of a number of planets."

Like the Copernican revolution, the Glorious Revolution of 1688–1689 had a profound influence on the future of Western societies. By deposing James II, William and his wife, Mary, ended the Stuart dynasty, a series of monarchs who had favored the Catholic Church and had limited the power of Parliament for decades. Under William and Mary, Parliament passed the Bill of Rights, which established the legislative supremacy of Parliament and barred Roman Catholics from the throne. These actions initiated the gradual process by which the power of the government of England shifted from the monarchy to Parliament, establishing a democratic system that would be copied, with some variations, by the United States and other democratic societies worldwide.

Whereas the Glorious Revolution had a major impact in the political sphere, the publication of Joyce's novel *Ulysses* represented a revolution in literature. In an effort to capture the sense of chaos and discontinuity that permeated the culture in the wake of World War I, Joyce did away with the use of straightforward narrative that had dominated fiction up to that time. The novel, whose structure mirrors that of Homer's *Odyssey*, combines realistic descriptions of events with passages that convey the characters' inner experience by means of a technique known as stream of consciousness, in which the characters' thoughts and feelings are presented without regard to logic or narrative order. Due to its departure from the traditional modes of fiction, *Ulysses* is often described as one of the seminal works of modernist literature. As stated by Pennsylvania State University professor Michael H. Begnal, "*Ulysses* is the novel that changed the direction of 20th-century fiction written in English."

Copernicus's theory of a sun-centered solar system, the Glorious Revolution, and James Joyce's *Ulysses* are just three examples of time-bound events that have had far-reaching effects—for better or worse—on the progress of human societies worldwide. History is made up of an inexhaustible list of such events. In the twentieth century alone, for example, one can isolate any number of world-shattering moments: the first performance of Igor Stravinsky's ballet *The Rites of Spring* in 1913; Japan's attack on Pearl Harbor on December 7, 1941; the launch of the satellite *Sputnik* on October 4, 1957. These events variously influenced the culture, society, and political configuration of the twentieth century.

Greenhaven Press's Events That Changed the World series is designed to help readers learn about world history by examining seemingly random events that have had the greatest influence on the development of cultures, societies, and governments throughout the ages. The series is divided into sets of several anthologies, with each set covering a period of one hundred years. Each volume begins with an introduction that provides essential context on the time period being covered. Then, the major events of the era are covered by means of primary and secondary sources. Primary sources include firsthand accounts, speeches, correspondence, and other materials that bring history alive. Secondary sources analyze the profound effects the events had on the world. Each reading is preceded by an introduction that puts it in context and emphasizes the event's importance in the ongoing evolution of world history. Additional features add to the value of the series: An annotated table of contents and an index allow readers to quickly locate material of interest. A chronology provides an easy reference for contextual information. And a bibliography offers opportunities for further exploration. All of these features help to make the Events That Changed the World series a valuable resource for readers interested in the major events that have shaped the course of humanity.

Revolutions Without Resolution

T he mere mention of the 1960s and 1970s calls up images of youthful protests and political involvement, expanding musical horizons, and very distinctive fashions and styles. A central theme of these two decades, however, was conflict, especially unresolved conflict.

In some prior decades in America, political conflict had rallied and unified the nation. In the 1950s it was the Cold War; in the 1940s, World War II; in the 1930s, the Great Depression; and in the 1910s, World War I. Although disagreement and dissent have always existed, Americans became deeply divided in the 1960s. In their book *America Divided: The Civil War of the 1960s*, Maurice Isserman and Michael Kazin remark,

> In the course of the 1960s, many Americans came to regard groups of fellow countrymen as enemies with whom they were engaged in a struggle for the nation's very soul. Whites versus blacks, liberals versus conservatives (as well as liberals versus radicals), young versus old, men versus women, hawks versus doves, rich versus poor, taxpayers versus welfare recipients, the religious versus the secular, the hip versus the straight, the gay versus the straight—everywhere one looked, new battalions took to the field, in a spirit ranging from that of redemptive sacrifice to vengeful defiance.[1]

This resentment, polarization, and sense of entitlement created an atmosphere of outrage and an attendant determination to right society's wrongs. From this determination sprang the civil rights movement, the women's movement, environmentalism, and protests of all kinds. Even by the end of the 1970s, most of these conflicts remained unresolved. Women and minorities still fought for equality and respect, and numerous issues—such as abortion, environmentalism, the Vietnam War, Watergate, the nature of patriotism, music, and appropriate means of protest—fueled heated debates.

The 1960s ushered in the nonviolent protest movement in the United States, a trend inspired by Mohandas Ghandi's prior work in other parts of the world. Many young people believed the government abused its power and allowed injustice, and they refused to comply. The first sit-in occurred in 1960 when a Woolworth's drug store refused to serve African Americans at its lunch counter. In response, a large group of students initiated a peaceful sit-in by taking all the seats in the dining area so no paying customers could comfortably be served. Similar protests took place throughout the 1960s, and some of America's finest leaders came from this movement, most notably Martin Luther King Jr. In *New Criterion*, Roger Kimball reflects on the 1960s protest movement:

> The Sixties also mean protest, the "youth culture" and a new permissiveness together with a new affluence: Dionysus with a bank balance and a cause. . . . In many respects, the Sixties really did amount to a counter-culture: a repudiation, an inversion of the Fifties—another period that lives on as a provocation. As we approach the end of the century and a new millennium, the question of what the Sixties wrought is far from settled. Indeed, it has lately assumed a new urgency as it becomes ever clearer that American culture is deeply riven along fault lines first defined by the reverberations of that long, percussive decade.[2]

Rebellion became increasingly common, and the youth of the 1960s questioned and challenged authority almost across the board. In *The Sixties: From Memory to History*, David Farber explains it this way:

> Young radicals in America in the 1960s, their numbers greatly expanded by a cold war struggle gone very sour in Vietnam, tended to see all of life's chances as infiltrated and even determined by the binds of the political. By politics they meant not simply the overt positions taken by elected officials or the partisan battles of Democrats and Republicans, but the elaborate structures used by all authorities—school administrators, corporate executives, doctors, members of the clergy, television producers—to shape what

was legitimate and what was deviant, what was debatable and what was not of collective concern.[3]

This distrust of authority had a basis in political events. When Saigon fell during the Vietnam War, it signaled the first time in history that America had entered a war and lost. Although American troops had been withdrawn by the time the North Vietnamese army captured Saigon and declared victory, the heavy American involvement had certainly not been forgotten. Add to that the Watergate fiasco, which revealed that the U.S. government, for all its maturity and fortitude, could be disgraced by its highest official. Even President Richard Nixon's supporters found it hard to defend him as facts about the illegal break-in of the Democratic headquarters came to light. To the rest of the world, America was as vulnerable to corruption as the regimes it so staunchly condemned.

Politics was not the only topic worthy of America's dissension. The introduction of the birth control pill in 1960 and the legalization of abortion in 1973 meant that women could take control of reproduction. The pill not only impacted the personal world of family and social life, it also changed women's roles as employees and professionals. Women could postpone childbirth for careers. Women became more in charge of their bodies, sexual behavior, families, and careers. Many in America did not see these changes as positive. Indeed, they blamed abortion and birth control for rising divorce rates and family breakdown.

Music, too, was a constant reflection of political and social dissent. In *America's Musical Pulse: Popular Music in Twentieth-Century Society*, Rudolf E. Radocy writes, "In the 1960s, many Americans, particularly older teenagers and people in their twenties, expressed their anti–Vietnam War sentiments with songs such as 'Give Peace a Chance,' 'Where Have All the Flowers Gone,' and 'Fixin' to Die Rag.' Other Americans protested the actions of war protesters with 'Okie from Muskogee.'"[4] In the same book, Jerome Rodnitzky contributed an essay about the changing role of music in the tumultuous 1960s:

> As the 1960's cultural revolution went on, the mood song replaced the message song. Increasingly, the music radiated general discontent and a vague antiestablishment mood, as opposed to focusing on specific evils. The political flavor was still there—if anything the fervor had increased—but the lyrics were no longer as

important, and they could seldom be heard over the music. The new psychedelic music registered a protest of form rather than substance. The music was sexual, highly creative, nonconformist, and clearly in protest of white middle-class America.[5]

The widespread context of dissent did not end in the 1960s and 1970s. Open dissent became a part of American identity. Debates over equal rights, abortion, and America's role in world politics still rage today.

Americans may have learned to channel their protest a bit more, however. During the 2003 war in Iraq, public opinion was divided about U.S. troop involvement. But American protesters were careful to direct their criticism not at the soldiers but at the war itself. Unlike Vietnam, American soldiers were treated with respect and a knowledge that they were risking their lives for the United States. Americans supported soldiers with widespread efforts to send letters and packages to those serving far from home. The success of those programs demonstrated a genuine feeling of support for the men and women in uniform. To be sure, this was not the experience of Vietnam veterans, who were called "baby killers" and spat upon when wearing a uniform in public.

In fact, in some ways, the 2003 war in Iraq reflected a return to previous, more unified decades. Protests of the war in Iraq were frowned upon as unpatriotic. Celebrities and other public figures were harshly criticized for speaking out against the war effort, despite the fact that, as of this writing, the reasons for entering the war (to disarm Saddam Hussein's weapons of mass destruction) had not materialized. Yet the public supplied new reason to support the war, the liberation of the oppressed Iraqi people. The more the public heard about the brutality of the Iraqi regime, the more Americans were proud to have participated in freeing the Iraqi people. While Americans continue to be deeply divided on social and cultural issues, the threat of terrorism has created a unification of feeling that has quieted their deep suspicions of government. The protests of the 1960s and 1970s perhaps left Americans a little more circumspect in rejecting any path that leads to a feeling of national security.

Notes

1. Maurice Isserman and Michael Kazin, *America Divided: The Civil War of the 1960s*. New York: Oxford University Press, 2000, p. 4.

2. Roger Kimball, "What the Sixties Wrought," *New Criterion*, March 1999, p. 14.

3. David Farber, *The Sixties: From Memory to History.* Chapel Hill: University of North Carolina Press, 1994, p. 3.

4. Rudolf E. Radocy, "Introduction: The Importance of Music to People," in *America's Musical Pulse: Popular Music in Twentieth-Century Society*, ed. Kenneth J. Bindas. Westport, CT: Praeger, 1992, p. xii.

5. Jerome Rodnitzky, "Popular Music as Politics and Protest," in *America's Musical Pulse: Popular Music in Twentieth-Century Society*, ed. Kenneth J. Bindas. Westport, CT: Praeger, 1992, p. 6.

American Women Before and After the Birth Control Pill

by Ann Marie Cunningham, Fran Snyder, and Nelly Edmondson Gupta

The birth control pill is a daily hormone pill that prevents pregnancy. The development of this pill and its widespread availability allowed women to reliably control pregnancy. Many women felt empowered by this new control over their bodies and their futures. The pill gained popularity very quickly through the course of the 1960s.

In addition to health and women's issues, moral and social issues surrounded the release of the birth control pill. Critics feared that the pill might increase premarital sex and promiscuity. Social commentators wondered how the pill might change the social lives of the younger generations. The new freedom enjoyed by young women meant that they could seriously pursue careers while delaying motherhood. Social commentators anticipated a slowing of population growth, as married couples used the pill to control the number of children they had. In short, one little pill represented an enormous amount of controversy.

In the following selection, originally published in 1990, Ann Marie Cunningham explores the impact of the pill on the lives of American women. She concludes that while the pill had some drawbacks, it has ultimately benefited women by increasing their freedom.

I n June 1960, the oral contraceptive was approved for sale—and transformed our lives like nothing before or since. The Pill, we called it, and everyone from teenage boys to country singers to eminent theologians knew just what we meant. In this age of AIDS, when the very idea of sexual revolution seems both archaic and dangerous, it's easy to forget how truly liberating the Pill seemed to be in 1960. Nothing else in the twentieth century—perhaps not even winning the right to vote—made such an immediate difference in women's lives. Overnight, the Pill gave women control of their reproductive systems; no longer was biology our absolute destiny.

Used properly, this contraceptive was virtually 100 percent effective, and it provoked profound social change. The Pill helped lower the birth rate and end America's baby boom in 1964. It spurred sexual frankness and experimentation. It allowed women to think seriously about careers because they could postpone childbirth. And it sparked the feminist and pro-choice movements; once women felt they were in charge of their own bodies, they began to question the authority of their husbands, their bosses, their doctors and their churches. As Founding Feminist Betty Friedan says today [in 1990]: "In the mysterious way of history, there was this convergence of technology that occurred just as women were ready to explode into personhood." Yet for many women, the Pill turned out to have a decidedly bitter aftertaste. The early versions were at best inconvenient and at worst dangerous, with alleged side effects ranging from dampened libido, depression and weight gain to blood clots, strokes and cancer.

Today's Pill is far safer, and 10.7 million American women now use it. It continues to be the nation's number-one method of birth control. But the profile of the Pill user has altered: Those now most likely to take it are aged fifteen to twenty-four.

Many of these young women, like their sixties' moms before them, regard taking the Pill as a rite of passage. "Most of my friends start the Pill when they begin going steady; it's part of a commitment you make," says Elizabeth, a twenty-two-year-old book editor from New York.

Some of the women who once shared that feeling now express a deep ambivalence, however. The Pill allowed Boomers to postpone childbearing for a long time—in some cases until they were too old to conceive. "I think maybe the Pill made us think we could turn our fertility on and off," says Jan, thirty-five, a college administrator from New Orleans who started taking the Pill as a teenager and decades later found herself unable to have a baby.

There are many other second thoughts about the Pill. Some women wonder if it didn't really do more for men, who availed themselves of the increased sexual opportunities while expecting women to automatically assume the responsibility for contraception. Says University of Washington sociologist Pepper Schwartz, "Since the Pill, men tend to assume that women will take care of protection."

The Development of the Pill

The Pill was developed by a team of Massachusetts-based researchers, including a Catholic physician, John Rock. Its biggest proponent was Margaret Sanger, the founder of the Planned Parenthood Federation of America. "No woman can call herself free who does not own and control her own body," she declared. Produced by the G.D. Searle pharmaceutical company and called Enovid, the original Pill combined synthetic forms of the hormones estrogen and progestin to suppress ovulation.

By 1965, six other companies were marketing their own brands of oral contraceptives. And by the end of the decade, nearly ten million women were taking the Pill, making it America's contraceptive of choice. But almost with its introduction, reports of serious problems began to surface, including blood clotting, heart disease, depression and strokes. After Congress held a hearing on the Pill's health effects, the Food and Drug Administration (FDA) forced manufacturers to include a package insert warning users of all possible side effects. Women heeded the caveats, and during the seventies usage dropped by 20 percent. Consumption recovered to present levels in the eighties, with the development of formulas containing as little as one fifth the estrogen and one twenty-fifth the progestin.

Sexual Dealings

The Pill's greatest effect may have been that it not only kept women from getting pregnant, it helped them change their sex lives. Finally, they could enjoy lovemaking wholeheartedly, without dreading the consequences. Says author Erica Jong, whose 1974 novel *Fear of Flying* was a textbook of sexual liberation, "Because women could control their fertility, they could start thinking of sexual pleasure instead of just pregnancy."

Most experts agree that the Pill contributed mightily to the sexual revolution. Effective forms of birth control—notably condoms—were already available, and sexual mores had begun to change in the postwar era. But the Pill made it easier for women to engage in sex more frequently. One 1965 study of married women who used oral contraceptives found that they had sex up to 39 percent more often than women using other methods of contraception.

birth control advocate
Margaret Sanger

And it encouraged public discussion of sex as well. For the first time, women's magazines could talk to their readers about sexual fulfillment, even headlining the word "orgasm" on their covers. Recalls Malcolm Potts, M.D., president of Family Health International, a nonprofit contraceptive-research organization, "You wouldn't mention condoms at cocktail parties, but you could talk about the Pill." And wisecracks about single women who were "on the Pill" were a shorthand for women who had stopped worrying about their reputations and started enjoying sex, just like men.

Here, too, however, the Pill brought mixed blessings. No longer were women looked on as fragile beings to be protected because they were vulnerable to pregnancy; instead they came to be regarded as independent equals who could—and should—take care of themselves. Gone were differentiations between "good girls" whom men would marry, and "bad girls" with whom they'd play around. "Before the Pill," says William Simon, Ph.D., professor of sociology at the University of Houston, "a woman who came prepared for contraception was making a statement about being prepared for sex which moved her to the slut end of the spectrum. The invisibility of the Pill muted that considerably." By the time the sexual revolution was at its height, many men expected women to have casual affairs and even one-night stands. "The key was that this was done without any expectation that it would end in marriage," says John Money, Ph.D., professor emeritus of medical psychology at Johns Hopkins University and Hospital, in Baltimore.

But while some female sexual behavior changed, attitudes did not always keep pace: Many women still wanted emotional as well as physical fulfillment. "One of the characteristics of women that remained true throughout all this was their inability to become sexually aroused without becoming emotionally attracted," says William Simon. "Men can go to bed with someone they don't necessarily like. That was never true of women." For the multitudes of women who did engage in no-strings sex, it soon became an empty exercise.

Nowadays, while we may take a certain degree of sexual frankness and freedom for granted, the excesses of the sixties seem emotionally empty and downright dangerous: We're haunted by AIDS, not to mention more than thirty other sexually transmitted diseases—against which the Pill is useless. In 1990, the social and sexual winds have shifted. Says Helen Singer Kaplan, Ph.D., a specialist in sexual disorders, "The Pill freed young men and women to have sex, but in 1990 the new fears are forcing them to learn to communicate, to put more energy into making their relationships work instead of seeking out more partners."

Difficult Questions

One change wrought by the Pill is still with us today: It raised women's expectations of their lives, and they soon were unwilling to bear a child if the pregnancy was accidental. "Having a baby when you didn't want a baby became unthinkable," says Rosalind Pollack Petchesky, professor of women's studies at Hunter College, in New York City. This attitude, Petchesky says, "undoubtedly contributed to the rise in abortions for women who did not use the Pill and sometimes for those who did."

For some women, the Pill's ramifications went beyond pregnancy and sex. Its reliability encouraged Catholic women to ignore the church's centuries-old prohibition against artificial birth control. Today, between 80 and 85 percent of Catholic women in the U.S. approve of the use of some form of contraception. For most U.S. Catholic women, using the Pill was their first significant rebellion against the church, and it meant that their attitude toward its teachings on other matters would never be quite the same. Says Rev. Andrew Greeley, the sociologist and author, "It has prompted them to question the church. They now make their own decisions on ethical and religious matters when they think the official church is wrong."

In some ways, the Pill has had as great an effect in the office as in the bedroom. In the early sixties, increasingly, numbers of women had already begun trickling into the job market. Their opportunities expanded just as the cost of living exploded, making it both more possible and essential for women to work. The Pill abetted these forces by allowing women for the first time to plan how they would mesh their new opportunities with their reproductive lives. As they did so, the birth rate fell until 1976, when Baby Boomers decided to conceive, creating the baby boomlet. Between 1970 and 1987, the rate of first births among women in their thirties more than doubled, according to the National Center for Health Statistics. For those aged forty to forty-four, it increased 75 percent.

The development of the birth control pill empowered women, giving them more control over their bodies and their futures.

If the Pill helped keep women in the office longer, it also may have made it easier for them to walk out of unsuccessful marriages. "The major influence on a woman's decision to leave her husband is probably whether she can find a job and support her family," says Pepper Schwartz. "But she is more likely to be able to leave if she has two children, not four.". . .

The Teenage Scene

Some parents and religious commentators worry that the Pill has encouraged adolescent promiscuity and teenage pregnancies. It's true that the rate of adolescent pregnancies in the United States, currently stable, remains the highest in the Western world. But a more likely culprit is lack of the Pill and of information about contraceptives. In 1988, the Alan Guttmacher Institute, the reproductive-health research organization in New York, found that U.S. women, especially teenagers, take the Pill less frequently than do women of other nationalities. One major reason: In the 1980s, state and federal cuts in social services severely limited teens' access to birth control and sex education. "We suffer from incredible ignorance about sexual matters in this country," says Louise Tyrer, M.D., vice-president of medical affairs for the Planned Parenthood Federation of America.

The Male Factor

In some ways, the Pill's very effectiveness has been unfortunate; American medical researchers have made little subsequent effort to develop a male contraceptive. But researchers have lagged on finding better birth-control methods for women as well. Today, this contraceptive gap is crucial, because the Pill cannot defend women against AIDS and sexually transmitted diseases that were no particular threat when it was invented. Says Susan C.M. Scrimshaw, Ph.D., professor of anthropology and public health at the University of California at Los Angeles, "In some cultures where AIDS is raging, women find it next to impossible to enlist their partners in using barrier methods." She calls on the drug industry to develop an entiviral spermicide that women could use without their partners' permission. "In a way," she adds, "it's appalling that after thirty years, the Pill is the best we have."

For all its shortcomings, however, the Pill brought the average American woman a degree of freedom that had previously been unimaginable. Given that freedom, women began to look more thoughtfully at sex, work, marriage, motherhood—and themselves. Even the Pill's considerable drawbacks prompted a new assertiveness: Women are now more willing to question their doctors and their drug companies. As a method of contraception, the Pill may be antiquated before the twenty-first century, but the power it conferred on women remains considerable, and its legacy enduring.

Expectations and Disappointments of the Bay of Pigs Invasion

by Maurice Halperin

The context of the Bay of Pigs, both prior to and after the invasion, is complicated and multifaceted. In addition to military and political issues, there were foreign affairs considerations. In the following excerpt, author Maurice Halperin provides some context for the decision to invade and the reactions to the invasion's failure.

Halperin's particular background gives him a unique perspective on this event. He was once a university professor and lecturer in America, Europe, and Latin America; his fields were American history, romance languages, economic geography, and political science. His background also includes alleged Communist sympathizing and sharing information with the Soviets, which resulted in an FBI investigation during the "Red scare" years of the early 1950s. When he refused to cooperate, he found himself unable to find work in the United States, so he began teaching abroad. The time he spent in Mexico, the Soviet Union, and Cuba led to several books and academic articles. Many believe that he was innocent of the charges

Maurice Halperin, *The Rise and Decline of Fidel Castro: An Essay in Contemporary History.* Berkeley: University of California Press, 1972. Copyright © 1972 by The Regents of the University of California. Reproduced by permission.

against him, but knowing the tense climate of the time, he opted to leave the country rather than face the futility of trying to clear his name. His years in the Soviet Union (1959–1962) and in Cuba (1963–1967) gave him a firsthand look at socialism, and he left both places unconvinced of its virtues.

Bay of Pigs Invasion Crushed

A few hours before dawn on Monday, April 17, [1961] Brigade 2506, consisting of 1,400 Cuban exiles fully equipped for battle, with an arsenal of weapons and equipment including artillery, tanks, and aircraft, began to disembark on two beaches in the Bay of Pigs, situated on the south coast of the island, about 140 miles southeast of Havana. A fierce battle began almost immediately and ended on Girón Beach in the late afternoon of Wednesday, April 19, less than seventy-two hours after the landing. The invasion was crushed and eventually close to 1,200 prisoners were rounded up. So rapidly had the action taken place that when word reached Washington that the brigade was in mortal danger, it was too late to provide effective help.

It seemed incredible that the mightiest power on earth, with the greatest experience of any nation in amphibious landings, could not secure a beachhead when, how, and where it wished on the well-mapped territory of a neighboring island in the throes of a profound social and economic reorganization and which had an immeasurably smaller military capability. Looked at in this way, the American defeat would appear to have been the result of monumental stupidity and colossal bungling. Yet it was not that simple.

Kennedy Criticized

On taking office, one of the first decisions President Kennedy had to make was whether or not to go ahead with the operation he had inherited from his predecessor. It is surprising to find how some otherwise competent scholars have misjudged the complexity of the problem Kennedy had to grapple with at this moment. For example, Professor Hans J. Morgenthau, [in *A New Foreign Policy for the United States*, Praeger, 1969] writes about "the fiasco of the Bay of Pigs" as follows:

The United States was resolved to intervene on behalf of its interests, but it was also resolved to intervene in such a way as not openly to violate the principle of non-intervention. . . . Had the United States approached the problem of intervening in Cuba in a rational fashion, it would have asked itself which was more important: to succeed in the intervention or to prevent a temporary loss of prestige among the uncommitted nations. Had it settled upon the latter alternative, it would have refrained from intervening altogether; had it chosen the former alternative, it would have taken all the measures necessary to make the intervention a success, regardless of unfavorable reactions in the rest of the world. Instead, it sought the best of both alternatives and got the worst.

The rationality suggested here presupposes the kind of situation Castro was in rather than the one Kennedy faced. Castro had to decide between the possibility of survival if he resisted and the certainty of nonsurvival if he did not. Kennedy had the more difficult task of matching a number of options and risks, of which the least was whether or not "to prevent a temporary loss of prestige among the uncommitted nations."

Options and Risks

In the months prior to the invasion, American policy toward Cuba had, on the one hand, drawn no significant support abroad and, on the other, had created a good deal of international apprehension. In this situation, military intervention in Cuba, whether successful or not, would inevitably entail a moral and political setback of varying dimensions for the United States in a considerable number of countries. However, in two areas, the repercussions could be of a different order of magnitude.

The Political Climate in Cuba

In Latin America, given the prevailing climate of nationalism and radicalism—that is to say, hostility to "Yankee imperialism"—and the considerable prestige of the Cuban Revolution at the time, it was entirely conceivable that an invasion of Cuba—especially with direct and open American participation—could set off disturbances that would seriously threaten American property and lives, undermine friendly governments, and generally set back relations between the "good neighbors" for years. As it was, even the more prudent type of invasion that took place set off scores of massive demonstrations with ominous potentialities, but which lost their momentum when Castro's victory was announced.

Then there was the question of the Soviet Union. That it had by then made a significant political and economic investment in Cuba was evident. How far it would go to protect its investment either directly or through countermeasures in other parts of the world, such as in Laos or West Berlin, were matters of conjecture; but they could not be lightly dismissed.

Fidel Castro, pictured above, became Cuba's leader in 1959 when he claimed power after the Cuban Revolution.

Thus, major risks, not only matters of prestige, were involved. To what extent were they worth taking? How urgent was it that Castro be destroyed? What were the real dimensions of the Communist menace in Cuba? Were there alternative ways of overcoming this menace? In the event of a successful invasion, what if Castro reverted to guerrilla warfare and held out for months or years in the mountains? What headaches would be faced in Cuba after Castro was eliminated?

President Kennedy's Dilemma

But Kennedy's situation was even more complicated. There was no time for a thorough study of all the pieces in these interlocking puzzles. The reason was that military action against Cuba had to be taken before May, when Castro's air force was due to be greatly strengthened with up-to-date Russian military aircraft manned by Cuban pilots trained in the Soviet Union. Finally, for Kennedy to conclude that the most "rational" decision under the circumstances would be to cancel the invasion almost certainly would have meant, at the very start of his administration, exposing himself and all he hoped to accomplish to a severe pounding from the Congress, the "military-industrial complex," the media, and a host of powerful political enemies. This was another risk that could not be brushed aside.

Kennedy's decision was to go ahead with the invasion on condition that the international political risks be reduced to a minimum. Given the fact that the preparations for the invasion had been widely publicized in the press, American involvement would be no secret; but this inconvenience could be managed if the direct participation of the armed forces of the United States was scrupulously avoided. Unprovoked direct aggression would be a flagrant violation of the United Nations Charter, as well as that of the OAS and of all international law. It would immediately whip up passions and place heavy pressures on foreign governments to take some action. Indirect aggression does not provoke the same urgent response. It can be denied, even if unconvincingly, or it can become entangled in the issues of a civil war. The debate over facts, allegations, motives, and credibility can be sufficiently complicated and lengthy, so that the sharpness of the question itself fades away. From the moral point of view, the distinction between direct and indirect aggression is slight; but in the marketplace of international politics the distinction is real.

The American Plan of Operations

Except for the Sunday morning quarterbacks analyzing Saturday's game with the benefit of hindsight, the invasion blueprint worked out by the Pentagon and the CIA, from the technical point of view, could be considered reasonably competent. The Bay of Pigs is a long, narrow body of water with several good beaches. The entrance to the Bay is from the south. In all other directions, the Bay is hemmed in by vast stretches of treacherous swampland. Between the eastern shore and the swampland there is a piece of dry land containing a sizable air strip and sufficient space for the brigade to assemble and set up its command headquarters. Access to the area by land at the time was limited to a couple of trails through the eastern swamps and to a single paved road that traversed the northern swamp, a stretch of about twenty miles. The entire zone was thinly populated, principally by charcoal makers and a few fishermen. It was a quiet and isolated spot, well suited for an inconspicuous landing.

According to the plan, once Castro's air force had been eliminated, the landing operations and the supporting vessels lying off shore would be immune to air attack. Paratroopers, supported by bombing and strafing of the brigade's B-26 planes, would be dropped far up the paved road, to be reinforced by artillery and tanks coming up from the beach, thus effectively sealing off the area. With a bridgehead secured, the Cuban Revolutionary Council, previously assembled in Miami, would be flown in and proclaimed as the provisional government of Cuba. What happened next would depend on the strength of supporting counterrevolutionary activity in various parts of the island and the extent to which Castro would be able to cope with the crisis. In any event, with a piece of Cuban territory firmly in the hands of the rump government, recognition could be extended by the United States and such assistance supplied as necessary to topple the Castro regime. . . .

Factors in Cuba's Favor

In February 1962 the Cuban government completed the publication of a four-volume report on the aborted invasion, entitled *Playa Girón: Derrota del Imperialismo* ("Girón Beach: Defeat of Imperialism"; the Cubans named the episode after the beach on which the final action occurred). The work contains some indispensable background, neglected by most foreign writers, for an

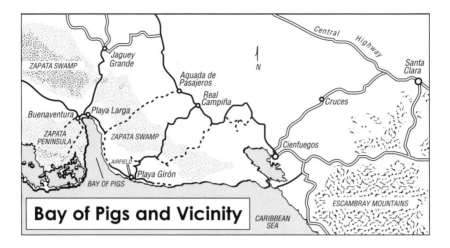

Bay of Pigs and Vicinity

understanding of what went wrong with the Pentagon-CIA plan. Particularly useful are sections of the more than 100 pages of the verbatim text of Fidel's television report, accompanied by a series of maps, delivered on April 21, two days after his victory.

Although the Bay of Pigs was, on the whole, well chosen as the site of the type of invasion contemplated, it was not without its drawbacks. To begin with, it was one of a number of locations that Fidel and his staff had considered likely in some degree to be selected by the invaders as a landing area. There was some element of chance in this coincidence but also of good judgment by those preparing to repel the invasion. Although Cuba has some 2,000 miles of irregular shoreline, there are only a limited number of sites that could be logically considered as suitable for the type of operation Castro had every reason to expect.

A matter the Pentagon-CIA might easily overlook, or to which they might attach small importance, was the fact that the charcoal makers of the area, one of the most impoverished segments of the Cuban population prior to the Revolution, had especially benefited from the Castro regime and were intensely loyal to it. In addition, there were some 200 "alphabetizers" working in the zone; and like all those participating in the literacy campaign, they were totally dedicated to the Revolution.

Setbacks to Invasion on the First Day

As a result of these factors, the invaders met with resistance from the moment the first landing craft approached the shore. The area was not fortified, but a day-and-night patrol had been on the lookout for several weeks. As soon as the landing occurred, and before the brigade could cut communications, the news was transmitted to an infantry battalion stationed at a sugar mill at the northern terminal of the paved road dissecting the swamp. At the same time, the local militia, consisting of several platoons of well-armed charcoal makers, went into action. Thus, the invaders lost some of the element of surprise, as well as the time required to subdue the militia.

A more important setback took place early in the morning of the same day when Castro's aviation, supposedly eliminated in Saturday's air strikes, appeared on the scene. What happened was that Fidel, anticipating an attempt to destroy his air force, had previously dispersed his dozen or so serviceable combat planes. At the same time, a number of permanently grounded planes were conspicuously lined up in close formation as decoys. The result was that relatively little damage was inflicted on Castro's real air power. As a matter of fact, as Castro claimed, his problem was that he had more planes than pilots.

Castro's Challenges and Successes

Another problem facing him was how to use his aviation; for although it included a couple of fast jet trainers while the enemy had only slower moving bombers, the latter outnumbered the planes Castro could put in the air at any one time. In addition, during the first day of fighting, Castro's infantry lacked antiaircraft equipment and from early morning on began to take severe punishment from enemy bombing and strafing.

Fidel's decision was to leave his infantry unprotected and attack the enemy flotilla. In this operation he lost two planes and two pilots, but succeeded in destroying a number of small craft, thereby disrupting the landing of men and supplies. He was also able to sink a 5,000-ton supply and communications vessel lying off shore. This was a hard blow to the invading force and later made escape by sea impossible, but it was not necessarily fatal. Castro did not achieve control of the air until the third day, and this was accomplished primarily by antiaircraft artillery which arrived only on the second day of battle. Meanwhile, the brigade's aviation, until it was eliminated, inflicted heavy casualties on Castro's troops and downed a number of his planes. Castro claimed that, at the rate his planes were being shot down, he would have lost all his pilots (who displayed exceptional courage and endurance) if the battle had lasted a short while longer.

Conflicting figures have been given concerning the exact number of casualties on each side. Nevertheless, all indications are that the killed and wounded on the government side out-numbered those of the brigade by a wide margin. Morale is an imponderable factor in war. Sometimes it can be decisive. In Castro's victory at the Bay of Pigs it undoubtedly played a very significant role. But Fidel and his staff must also be given credit, beginning with the day-and-night training of artillery recruits months before the invasion, for effective planning and use of limited resources. In any battle, or ping-pong match for that matter, victory or defeat does not depend on only one of the contestants. . . .

Significance of the Event

From the point of view of the Cuban Revolution, except for the heavy casualties, the Bay of Pigs incident could not have turned out any better. Cuba's international prestige zoomed upward. National pride soared and with it popular confidence in Fidel's leadership. Counterrevolution on the island received a setback from which it never recovered. In later and more difficult years, the memory of the victory, assiduously kept alive by the regime, would serve to bolster a sometimes lagging spirit of nationalism and enthusiasm for the Revolution among the Cuban people.

Does this mean that, from the point of view of the United States, it could not have turned out any worse? Nobody can say what might have occurred had Brigade 2506 succeeded in establishing and maintaining a bridgehead. As good a guess as any is that the United States would have become involved in a nasty and protracted civil war, with unpredictable consequences. Equally unpredictable would have been the course of events had there been open and direct American military intervention to guarantee the success of the invasion. The only thing hindsight reveals with unimpeachable logic is that no invasion would have been better than the one that took place.

Looking back dispassionately, the underlying miscalculation of Kennedy, his political experts, and his military planners was an underestimation of the enemy's capacity to resist, a failure to take into account the military capability that the leadership of a technically deficient but aroused and highly motivated society can frequently generate out of its limited material and human resources. It was a historically and culturally conditioned error, and particularly so in the context of inter-American relations—the kind a great power can make when it undertakes to apply punitive measures against a small, backward nation. It was, in part, the same error that turned the American intervention in Vietnam into a savage war of unexpected dimensions and tragic futility.

Eisenhower's Notes on Discussion with Kennedy About the Bay of Pigs Fiasco

by Dwight D. Eisenhower

On April 17, 1961, a group of Cuban exiles, trained and funded by the U.S. Central Intelligence Agency (CIA), invaded Cuba to overthrow Castro's regime. The invasion was a disaster; three days later the Cuban military had captured 1,179 of the invaders and killed the other 274. The failure of the Bay of Pigs invasion was a black eye on John F. Kennedy's presidency. It was a military and political embarrassment, and the young president faced an uphill battle to restore his credibility both at home and abroad.

On April 22 Kennedy met with his predecessor, Dwight D. Eisenhower, to explore the reasons for the invasion's failure. The following transcript reveals some of the content of that discussion, as a beleaguered young president and a respected military leader review the event.

Kennedy was born on May 29, 1917. He was the second of nine children. In World War II, he distinguished himself as a brave and tenacious commander in the navy. After the war he won a seat in the

Dwight D. Eisenhower, Notes on Luncheon Meeting, April 22, 1961, Eisenhower Library, Papers, Post-Presidential, 1961–1969, Box 11: Kennedy, John F., 1962.

House of Representatives in 1946 and a Senate seat in 1952. In 1953 he married Jacqueline Lee Bouvier. After a hard-fought campaign and a narrow victory over Richard Nixon, Kennedy won the presidency in 1960. A few short months later, he faced the disastrous Bay of Pigs invasion. Much of his focus shifted from domestic affairs to international concerns as relations with the Soviets and with Southeast Asia intensified. Although Kennedy made progress with some of his domestic programs, his efforts were cut short on November 22, 1963, when he was assassinated in Dallas, Texas.

Eisenhower was born on October 14, 1890. He was one of six sons. In 1911 he entered the U.S. Military Academy at West Point, where he was an above-average student and athlete. He graduated in 1915 and married Mamie Doud the following year. During World War I he longed for combat but was valued too highly as a trainer. He stayed in the army through the Great Depression and was valued for his experience and credentials. In 1940 he got the chance to be a field commander and excelled. After the bombing of Pearl Harbor, he advised top decision makers on Capitol Hill and earned important commands in World War II, including the invasion of Normandy. His popularity among Americans skyrocketed, and he won two presidential terms (1952 and 1956). He died in 1969 after suffering several heart attacks.

Mr. Kennedy met me when I landed from the helicopter at Camp David. We went to the terrace at Aspen Cottage to talk. He began by outlining the Cuban situation, including a description of the planning, the objectives and the anticipated results. This outline agreed exactly with that given me by [head of CIA] Allen Dulles yesterday morning.

Problems and Mistakes in Cuba

He explained in detail where things began to go awry and stated that the whole operation had become a complete failure. Apparently some men are still hiding in the "bosque" and possibly have made their way to the mountains. Apparently about 400 prisoners were taken.

The chief apparent causes of failure were gaps in our intelligence, plus what may have been some errors in ship loading, timing, and tactics.

The disastrous Bay of Pigs invasion was a military and political embarrassment for President John F. Kennedy.

It appears that too much specialized equipment was carried in a single ship and, when this ship was damaged, the troops on the beach were left fairly helpless. I inquired whether or not the troops had had the equipment immediately with them (in platoons and companies) to establish effective road blocks on the three avenues of entry into the swamp area. He was under the impression that this equipment was properly distributed and the troops well trained in its use. Therefore the reason for the quick penetration of the swamp into the vulnerable beachhead was unknown.

The press has mentioned a great deal about MIGs [military aircraft]. The President is not certain, and neither was Allen Dulles, that these were MIGs. They could easily have been T-33s, equipped with rockets and guns; but, at least, they shot down a number of our airplanes and apparently operated effectively against our troops in the beachhead.

Seeking Improved Future Performance

He is having General Taylor come to Washington to analyze all phases of the operation, including all of the planning and the methods so as to see whether there are lessons to be learned. He has the feeling that we can be faced with some similar situation over the next decade and thinks we should do our best to be prepared to meet it. (He did not say that this report would be made public—but I did get the impression that it would.)

The next thing that he wanted to talk about were the direction and prospects for future action. I was unable to give him any detailed suggestions, but did say that I would support anything that had as its objective the prevention of Communist entry and solidification of bases in the Western hemisphere.

Concerns About Communist Military Superiority

He believes that the two great powers have now neutralized each other in atomic weapons and inventories; but that in numbers of troops, and our exterior communications as opposed to the interior communications of the Communists, we are relatively weak.

He did not seem to think that our great seapower counteracted this situation completely.

The only real suggestion I could give him regarding the Western Hemisphere was to do his very best to solidify the OAS [Organization of American States] against Communism, including a readiness to support, at least morally and politically, any necessary action to expel Communist penetration. I said that this was something that had to be worked on all the time. I told him, also, that I believed the American people would never approve direct military intervention, by their own forces, except under provocations against us so clear and so serious that everybody would understand the need for the move.

Final Overview of Bay of Pigs Errors

The President did not ask me for any specific advice. I contented myself with merely asking a few questions about the tactical action, including the timing of the support that I understood the Navy Air had given to the landings. He said that in the first instance they were so anxious to keep the United States hand concealed that they accorded no such support, and when they finally did get word of its need it was too late. This situation was complicated by the fact that all communications went out. I understood that the communication equipment was on the ship that sank, but this is hard to believe because each unit carries some light communication equipment, including the ability to send ra-diograms to a distance of some fifty to a hundred miles.

There are certainly factors, now unknown, that will finally come to light under searching scrutiny. The purpose of this scrutiny is not to find any scapegoat, because the President does seem to take full responsibility for his own decision, but rather to find and apply lessons for possible future action.

An American Diplomat Stationed in Berlin Recalls the Issues Surrounding the Wall

by Howard Trivers

After World War II, Germany's capital city, Berlin, was a city ideologically divided. Although postwar agreements determined that Berlin was inside Russia's zone, its standing as the capital city also required that France, Britain, and the United States occupy it. This presented numerous problems as opposite cultures and political philosophies struggled to cohabit in a single city. By the early 1960s the growing issue of refugees escaping Communist Europe through Berlin was a concern of Soviet leader Nikita Khrushchev. In August a checkpoint was established to curb this problem, and the Berlin Wall soon replaced the original barbed-wire fence.

Howard Trivers was in Berlin at the time, serving as an American diplomat in Germany. He had made a career in foreign service, honing his skills at political negotiations and international conferences. During his years in Berlin, he was an active participant in the events

---

Howard Trivers, *Three Crises in American Foreign Affairs and a Continuing Revolution*. Carbondale: Southern Illinois University Press, 1972, pp. 21–56. Copyright © 1972 by Southern Illinois University Press. Reproduced by permission.

surrounding the building of the wall. He worked directly with other advisers from Great Britain, France, and West Berlin, and he maintained communication with Soviet advisers. In short, he knew the real stories of what was happening during this historical time in world history.

In the following excerpt, Trivers offers a historical rendering of the Berlin crisis, told more than a decade later. His account is detailed and thorough, presented in the matter-of-fact tone of a government official. At the same time, he interjects his personal recollections and impressions, giving the reader an insider's point of view on the event.

Early Contrasts Between East and West Berlin

Why did the Communists find it necessary in the summer of 1961 to build the Wall? In the spring of 1958, Anastas Mikoyan [President of the Soviet Union] had visited East Berlin and taken occasion to look around West Berlin at the same time.

Struck by the contrast between West Berlin and East Berlin, he gave [Walter] Ulbricht [the Communist leader of the German Democratic Republic] "unshirted hell," saying that the East Germans should remove finally the World War II rubble, clean up East Berlin and rebuild the center of the city in order to make it a "show window" of the Socialist camp able to outshine West Berlin, the "show window" of the West. About this time Khrushchev was making his boasts about the Soviet Union's surpassing the United States in per capita production in a few years and Ulbricht was imitating him by claiming that the GDR [German Democratic Republic] would surpass the Federal Republic in per capita production of consumer goods by 1961.

What was the situation in East Germany in 1961? The forced collectivization in the spring of 1960 had led to a sharp decline in agricultural production and great resentment in the countryside. Consumer shortages and maldistribution had led to worker apathy and a decrease in productivity. Communist pressure on the church, in education, and in cultural matters had further alienated the intellectuals. In 1960, ten percent of the East German doctors fled to the West. There is a story which is very revealing about the situation at the time in the GDR. The flight of physicians had been so alarming that the East German regime had imposed special controls on, and police surveillance of, doctors. As a result, in one rural district from which five physicians endeavored to flee, four were caught by the police and only one escaped with his entire family. The four who were caught had sold some of their possessions (one had sold his house, another had sold his car) or had withdrawn money from banks or bought diamonds, etc. The one who was successful in escaping with his family was the one who bought a new house, redecorated it, and moved into it three weeks before he left. He was thereafter not watched and he brought his entire family out, albeit with just a few small valises. He left much behind, but accomplished his escape.

Pre-Wall Panic in East Berlin

There is a certain irony in the fact that the Berlin crisis which had been initiated by Khrushchev in November 1958 in order to drive the Western Allies out of Berlin had the effect instead of driving East Germans out of the Communist German Democratic Republic. Khrushchev's Berlin crisis had increasingly stirred up and worried East Germans who had followed the ups and downs of the ultimatums and threats and quieting statements from November 1958 on. The renewal of Khrushchev's threatening demands in the winter and spring of 1961 once more served to stimulate a high rate of refugee flights. There was a growing *Torschlusspanik*—that marvelously expressive German word which in this context means "panic from fear that the escape hatch would be closed." Press reports about the Berlin discussions at the Kennedy-Khrushchev meeting in Vienna on June 4, the Soviet release on June 10 of the *aide-mémoire* Khrushchev had given to Kennedy on June 4, Khrushchev's television speech on June 15 reasserting his ultimative demands before the Soviet people, and strong accompanying statements by Ulbricht had the effect of bringing on the panic with full force. In July 1961 more than 30,000 East Germans came over as refugees into West Berlin—nearly twice the previous monthly average. The East German authorities made frantic efforts to stop the refugee flight through more frequent checks and interrogations. They introduced measures to oblige some 50,000 East Berliners working in West Berlin to give up their jobs. They supported these measures with an intensive propaganda campaign, ranging from branding refugees as "traitors" to inventing a "polio epidemic" in West Germany. They probably succeeded in blocking or restraining the flight of many thousands, but they could not stem this panic tidal flow. More than 22,000 refugees arrived in West Berlin in the first twelve days of August.

East and West Berlin Officially Sever

The Wall signified the failure of Ulbricht's "show window" effort, a demonstration that the Communists could not win in open, honest competition with the capitalist West. What did the Wall accomplish for the Communists? It stopped the refugee flow; it broke contacts between East and West Germans; it halted the role of West Berlin as a meeting place for all Germans; and it made easier the economic and political development of the GDR as a separate Communist state in the Eastern European pattern.

Why did the Western Allies permit the building of the Wall? There were many reproaches at the time, and we who were involved there tended to search our souls and reproach ourselves as well. However, we recognized that Berlin had been divided into four sectors by the Four Power agreements going back to 1944–45. The city became effectively divided, albeit without a wall, at the time of the Berlin blockade and the airlift in 1948–49. Thereafter there was a separate currency, a separate administration, an Eastern-oriented economy in East Berlin, the Soviet sector. East Berlin had been under Communist control for sixteen years. On the other hand, it is true that there had been freedom of movement within the city during all this period; even during the Berlin blockade, 1948–49, free movement between the sectors of Berlin had continued unimpeded. Moreover, this freedom of movement within the city was grounded in explicit agreements with the Soviets. On July 7, 1945, in a meeting in Berlin between General Clay and Marshall Zhukov, it was agreed that transportation and movement within Berlin were to be unrestricted between the sectors. This right of free movement had been confirmed by practice, and was likewise supported by interpretation of the May 4, 1949 quadripartite agreement which terminated the Berlin blockade, and by the June 1949 agreement of the Four Power Council of Foreign Ministers. By construction of the Wall and the attendant restrictions on free movement between East and West Berlin, the Soviets and the East German Communists were thus acting in direct violation of Allied rights.

Should the Western Allies have moved in on August 13 to re-move the barbed wire? General Clay, who came to Berlin five weeks later and stayed through the winter until early May, thought that perhaps it might have been done successfully within the first twenty-four hours. No one who has ever worked for this extraordinary man would dispute his view lightly. If General Clay had been there on August 13, it might have been different, but I honestly doubt it. When General Clay at the time of the Berlin blockade in 1948–49 was the American Military Gover-nor for all of Germany, he reported directly to the Army chief of staff in Washington, and through his political adviser, Robert Murphy, directly to the Secretary of State. In 1961, the United States commander in Berlin, a major general, was at the end of a command line with two headquarters echelons between him and Washington; he reported first to Army headquarters in Hei-delberg, from there to the U.S. commander of NATO forces in Paris, and then to Washington. In any case General Clay would have had to seek authorization for any action, and in my opinion he never would have received the authorization, just as he never received the authorization he requested to push an armed convoy through the Soviet zone to Berlin to break the surface route blockade in July 1948.

Furthermore, it must be borne in mind that the barbed wire was not directly on the sector boundary; it was well on the East-ern side. To remove the barbed wire we would have had to cross the sector line into an area which had been under Soviet and Communist control for more than fifteen years. Moreover, the sector line on the Western side was divided into three compo-nents: American, British, and French. Any action to be effective would have had to be a joint Allied action. To obtain authoriza-tion for prompt action from three governments was hardly pos-sible. The French commandant was under the very strict control of the French Foreign Office; he did not even have authority to send a protest letter to the Soviet commandant without the spe-cific approval of the text by Paris, and there were standing in-structions in the Quai d'Orsay that no policy message to the French commandant could be sent without the personal approval of French Foreign Minister Couve de Murville. The British com-mandant had a little more leeway than the French, but he cer-tainly would have needed authorization from London before taking any action. As a matter of fact, the British commandant was under instructions from the highest authority in London not to move any of his troops out of his sector into another sector without the prior approval of the other commandant. If the British troops were to engage in joint maneuvers with the Americans in our sector, the British had to make a formal request to our commandant for permission for their troops to enter the American sector. The Soviet commandant certainly would not have given such permission—least of all on August 13, 1961.

The East German armed forces and police were at the barbed wire. If we had crossed the line to remove the barbed wire, I am convinced that they would not have sought to resist. They would have moved back two hundred or four hundred yards and commenced to rebuild the barbed wire fence there. They were committed and they would have had to do it. We would then have been obliged to keep moving in farther and farther into the Soviet sector in order to remove the barbed wire, giving thus the appearance of aggression on our part.

There was another factor cautioning inaction on our part, perhaps the most important one. In the center of the city near the main Friedrichstrasse railroad station and the major crossing points into West Berlin, there were thousands of East Germans who had come from the Soviet Zone into the city on that day with the intention of going over to West Berlin. These thousands were milling around behind the East German army contingents. On the Western side, moreover, there were thousands of West Berliners watching what was going on at the sector line. A spark could have caused a conflagration in the form of a popular uprising as on June 17, 1953 which would have brought out the Soviet tanks again—with unforeseeable consequences. The German city authorities and the Allies as well recognized this great danger. . . .

There is another basic reason why the Allied commandants in Berlin did not seriously consider taking forceful action against the erection of the Wall, nor even request authorization for such action. The foreign ministers of the United States, Britain, France, and West Germany had met in Paris August 5–7, primarily to discuss the Berlin situation. The main outcome of the meeting was agreement on three vital issues regarding Berlin over which the Allies were ready to go to war, if necessary. All three vital issues were related to *West* Berlin only. These three vital issues, which were leaked to the Paris *Herald Tribune* at the time, were to uphold Allied rights in West Berlin, to ensure the economic viability of West Berlin, and to maintain free access to and from West Berlin. The three Allied commandants in Berlin were aware of this tripartite understanding, and this agreed policy explains to a considerable extent their reaction to the Wall, as well as the reaction in Washington, London, and Paris. . . .

Solidarity Emerges from Tension

Tension in Berlin over the years has brought about a feeling of solidarity among the Western Allies and the West Berliners. There is a special breed of U.S. government military and civilian officials called Alt-Berliner ("old Berliners"), numbering in the thousands. Their distinction is that they have all served in Berlin in the American military or civilian establishment sometime after 1945, and their lives have become associated with the people of that city and their survival in freedom. When Berlin is threatened, the old Berliners stir and become active. The measures which the Kennedy administration took to shore up West Berlin morale at the time of the Wall were, assuredly, the result of the obscure and energetic push of the old Berliners scattered in large numbers in key positions throughout Washington officialdom. There is doubtless a similar special breed of old Berliners in London and Paris, smaller in number because the British and French establishments in Berlin have been smaller than the American. One of the unique pleasures of diplomatic work in Berlin was to experience not only the congeniality of British and French colleagues living under the same stress, but also the generally common viewpoints on basic issues. We three political advisers rarely had difficulty in coming to a mutual understanding among ourselves, nor did we often find differences with our superiors in Berlin. The problem was to gain acceptance of a common viewpoint from our respective capital cities, and we each tended to feel ourselves more often in opposition to our own capital than to our Berlin colleagues, experiencing thus the solidarity of field officers obliged by circumstances to work in common, over against separate headquarters, each of which viewed the problems from varying premises and preconceptions.

This sense of solidarity was not limited to the Western Allies, but it encompassed the West Berliners as well. In a sense, we were all in the same boat, or rather in the same trap, surrounded by twenty-three Soviet army divisions. The Allied military forces were token, a trip wire for general war; our security depended on the steadfastness of our government, or rather on the Soviet perception of our government's steadfastness. There is a strong human solidarity born of threat and there can be a transnational loyalty as evidenced by the following. Each October the West Berlin police held in the giant Olympic stadium a Polizeischau (a police exhibition). There was marching, acrobatics on motorcycles, demonstrations of police dog training, etc. The stadium was always packed with Berliners, West and East, and one section was reserved for the occupation authorities and their families. The American, British, and French armies each provided a band for the occasion, as did the German police. The army bands first marched separately playing national tunes, followed by the German band. Each band was greeted enthusiastically by the Berlin audience. However, the high point of the day always came when the three Allied army bands marched together with the West Berlin police band playing the tune of "Die Berliner Luft," which had somehow become the anthem of the city. At that moment there was always an emotional stirring which gripped the Berliners and the Allies alike in response to this symbol of their joint resistance to a common threat.

The Atmosphere in West Berlin Relaxes

As to be expected of an old Berliner, powered by nostalgia, in May 1967 I returned to Berlin for a visit, the first since we had left at the end of February in 1962. I went and came back on the military train from Frankfurt to Berlin as I formerly used to travel. I spent a week in the city. How different was the atmosphere! So relaxed on the train, at the military headquarters, in the State Department Mission, among the Berlin population. Everything seemed thriving, prosperous. How different the atmosphere in Berlin was then from the time of tension before and immediately after the Wall was built.

The Wall represented the failure of the Communist "show window" policy, but it also represented the failure of the Communist effort to force the Western Allies out. We who were in Berlin when the Wall was built did not then recognize that the Wall meant the end of the crisis, the end of Soviet threats and ultimata. After a period of adjustment to the fact of the Wall, after the initial period of flights and dramatic shootings at the Wall, the situation in the divided city quieted down. By the fall of 1962, the

Berlin crisis was over; not over by agreement, the Soviet push just stopped.

Why did the Soviet push stop? Partly the Wall, by halting the refugee flow, bringing about a reluctant acquiescence of the East German population in their lot, and introducing a Communist-type frontier through the divided city, made the continuing presence of a free West Berlin as an enclave in the Communist realm more tolerable to the Soviets; partly the Cuba missile crisis, partly the downfall of Khrushchev and the advent of a less venturesome collective leadership—more importantly, the Soviet rift with Communist China, and the concomitant Soviet fear of conflict on two fronts brought the consequent need to quiet down friction points with the West and to seek a *status quo* settlement on the basis of a divided Europe.

Publication of Rachel Carson's *Silent Spring:*
1962

Carson's Early Pioneer Work in the Field of Environmentalism

by Ralph H. Lutts

The social impact of Rachel Carson's *Silent Spring* was enormous and is, by extension, still felt today. In this essay Ralph H. Lutts explores the social and scientific context for Carson's book and explains why the information in the book was so alarming to the American public. He describes the hopes and fears of people living in the new atomic age and how this affected their reception of Carson's claims. Politics, entertainment, consumerism—all of these felt the effects of *Silent Spring.*

Lutts earned his degree in biology from Trinity University and his doctorate in education from the University of Massachusetts and is now a professor of environmental history. He has taught at Hampshire College, Goddard College, the University of Virginia, and Virginia Tech. For an article he wrote for *Environmental History*, he won the Forest History Society's Ralph W. Hidy Award. In addition to his scholarly articles, he wrote the book *The Nature Fakers: Wildlife, Science, and Sentiment* (1990) and edited *The Wild Animal Story* (1998). His dedication to his field extends to national efforts, as he is the president of the American Nature Study Society and serves as a board member on numerous environmental education

Ralph H. Lutts, "Chemical Fallout: Silent Spring, Radioactive Fallout, and the Environmental Movement," *And No Birds Sing: Rhetorical Analysis of Rachel Carson's Silent Spring*, edited by Craig Waddell. Carbondale: Southern Illinois University Press, 2000. Copyright © 1985 by Ralph H. Lutts. Reproduced by permission.

organizations. Lutts actively seeks out an interdisciplinary approach to his subject matter, both in writing and in the classroom.

Silent Spring Initiates Environmentalism

The landmark book *Silent Spring* played a vitally important role in stimulating the contemporary environmental movement. Never before or since has a book been so successful in alerting the public to a major environmental pollutant, rooting the alert in a deeply ecological perception of the issues, and promoting major public, private, and governmental initiatives to correct the problem. It was exceptional in its ability to combine a grim warning about pesticide poisoning with a text that celebrated the living world. *Silent Spring* has been compared in its social impact to *Uncle Tom's Cabin* (United States. Cong. Senate. Subcommittee on Reorganization and International Organizations of the Committee on Government Operations. Interagency Coordination in Environmental Hazards (Pesticides). 88th Cong., 1st sess. 1964, pt. 1. Washington: GOP, 1964.) ; John Kenneth Galbraith described it as one of the most important books of Western literature (*New York Times Book Review*, June 3, 1979, p. 13); and Robert Downs listed it as one of the "books that changed America" (book of same name, 1970, pp. 260–61).

Rachel Carson's case against the indiscriminate use of pesticides prevailed in the face of powerful, well-financed opposition by the agricultural and chemical industries. Despite this opposition, she prompted national action to regulate pesticides by mobilizing a concerned public. The book established a broad constituency for addressing the problem—broader, perhaps, than that enjoyed by any previous environmental issue. Never before had so diverse a body of people—from bird-watchers, to wildlife managers and public-health professionals, to suburban home owners—been joined together to deal with a common national and international environmental threat. Her success in the face of what might have been overwhelming opposition suggests there was something significantly different between the response to *Silent Spring* in 1962 and the pesticide-control efforts of the first half of the century.

The issue of pesticide pollution was not new. Since the introduction of Paris green around 1867, highly toxic compounds of lead and arsenic were widely used in agriculture despite the significant health hazards they presented. As one example, seventy-five million pounds of lead arsenate were applied within the United States in 1944; eight million pounds were even used in the 1961–62 crop year when DDT was preeminent. In the early decades of their use, these toxic chemicals could sometimes be found as visible coatings on farm produce in retail markets. Over the years, stories of acute poisonings and warnings of the dangers of chronic toxicity appeared in the press. Everyone was warned to scrub or peel fruits and vegetables before they were eaten. Many public-health officials attempted to institute strong regulations and strict residue tolerances, but the general public, medical profession, and agriculture industry showed only limited concern. This relative indifference to the hazards of pesticides in the first half of the century stands in stark contrast to the vocal outcry following the publication of *Silent Spring*.

Why is it that the book's publication in 1962 had such a major impact upon the public? The answer to this question might reveal a great deal about the origins of contemporary environmental concerns, but no one has examined it systematically. A number of answers have been suggested, focusing most often upon Carson's extraordinary skill and reputation as a writer, the general circumstances surrounding the rise of pesticide use and misuse, the publisher's marketing strategy, and the chemical industry's response. Many authors have also noted the growing public awareness of a variety of environmental problems, including water and air pollution. One of the major events to bring the hazards of pesticides to public attention was the "cranberry scare" of 1959 when people were warned against eating this traditional fruit during the Thanksgiving season because of pesticide contamination. The thalidomide syndrome also came to the public's attention shortly before the publication of *Silent Spring*, and the pictures of the distorted infant limbs caused by a supposedly beneficial drug certainly made people pay greater attention to Carson's message (*The House of Life: Rachel Carson at Work*, 1972, p. 261; *Since Silent Spring*, 1970, pp. 50–51; *Scientific American*, 1962, pp. 29–35).

There was another issue, however, that played an equal or greater role in preparing the public to accept Carson's warning— an issue that has been largely overlooked. She was sounding an alarm about a kind of pollution that was invisible to the senses;

could be transported great distances, perhaps globally; could accumulate over time in body tissues; could produce chronic, as well as acute, poisoning; and could result in cancer, birth defects, and genetic mutations that may not become evident until years or decades after exposure. Government officials, she also argued, were not taking the steps necessary to control this pollution and protect the public. Chemical pesticides were not the only form of pollution fitting this description. Another form, far better known to the public at the time, was radioactive fallout. Pesticides could be understood as another form of fallout.

People in the United States and throughout the world were prepared, or preeducated, to understand the basic concepts underlying Rachel Carson's *Silent Spring* by the decade-long debate over radioactive fallout preceding it. They had already learned that poisons, in this case radioactive ones, could create a lasting global danger. . . .

Strontium 90

> Oh where, oh where has the fallout gone,
> Oh where can the poison be,
> Why right in the milk and the other things
> That the milkman brings to me.

Sen. George Aiken (Rep., VT) was displeased with this and other songs sung by "certain pacifist groups." In 1962, he asked a congressional hearing witness whether he did not think "it was a great calamity that the critics of the use of milk and other dairy products did not advise the Maker before He set up the original milk program?" The senator's pique was prompted by the universal presence of strontium 90 in milk products, the resulting public anxiety regarding their wholesomeness, and the tremendous emotional leverage that the fear of radioactive milk gave the opponents of nuclear weapons.

A radioactive isotope, strontium 90 (Sr-90) has a half-life of twenty-eight years, making it a long-lasting component of fallout. Soon after World War II, the Atomic Energy Commission (AEC) recognized that Sr-90, which is chemically similar to calcium, can accumulate in bones and possibly lead to cancer (*Bulletin of the Atomic Scientists*, April 1949, p. 119). In August 1953, its presence in animal bones, milk, and soil was first confirmed by the Lamont Geological Observatory. Lamont established a worldwide network for sampling human bone, and within a few years found Sr-90 present in "all human beings, regardless of age or geographic locations." Sr-90 found its way into humans via the ecological food chain, as fallout in the soil was picked up by plants, further concentrated in herbivorous animals, and eventually consumed by humans. . . .

These and other studies, and the wide publicity they received, brought the issue of radioactive fallout very close to home. No longer was fallout a problem limited to a few Japanese fishermen or western ranchers. People around the nation knew that invisible radioactive material was in the air they breathed and lodged within their own and their children's bones. In learning about this hazard they also learned about the ecological food chain, the biological concentration of these materials, and the cancer and other radiation-induced effects that might strike them in future years. . . .

Chemical Fallout

Silent Spring was published on 27 September 1962—one month before the Cuban missile crisis and one year before the signing of the Limited Test Ban Treaty; almost three years after the release of the film version of *On the Beach* and two years before the release of Stanley Kubrick's *Dr. Strangelove: Or, How I Learned to Stop Worrying and Love the Bomb.* The nation was steeped in years of debate about nuclear weapon and fallout, which served as a point of reference to help people understand the hazards of pesticides and as a fearful symbol to motivate action.

The environmental and health hazards of radioactive materials were on Rachel Carson's mind as she wrote the book. In the summer of 1960, while deeply involved in writing *Silent Spring*, she also worked on a revised edition of *The Sea Around Us.* In a new preface, she wrote about the impact of fallout and of the ocean disposal of nuclear wastes upon the marine environment. She described how marine organisms can concentrate radioisotopes and wrote, "By such a process tuna over an area of a million square miles surrounding the Bikini bomb test developed a degree of radioactivity enormously higher than that of the sea water." In creating these materials, she warned, we must face the question of whether we "can dispose of these lethal substances without rendering the earth uninhabitable" (xi–xiii).

It is no accident, then, that the first pollutant Carson mentioned by name in *Silent Spring* was not a pesticide but strontium 90. Well known to the American public, Sr-90 was a tool to help her explain the properties of pesticides. Early in *Silent Spring* she wrote:

> Strontium 90, released through nuclear explosions into the air, comes to earth in rain or drifts down as fallout, lodges in soil, enters into the grass or corn or wheat grown there, and in time takes up its abode in the bones of a human being, there to remain until his death. *Similarly*, chemicals sprayed on croplands or forests or gardens lie long in soil, entering in a chain of poisoning and death. (6, emphasis added) . . .

Similarities Between Fallout and Pesticides

I am not suggesting that using fallout as an analogy for pesticides was a central part of the design of this very sophisticated book. As a thoughtful person who was aware of the issues of her time, however, it was impossible for Carson not to have been influenced by the decade of public discussion and debate. Both Carson and her editor, Paul Brooks, were well aware of the similarities between the effects of fallout and pesticides. And while, when interviewed nearly twenty-two years after publication of *Silent Spring*, Brooks did not recall that this was a major part of their conversation (Brooks, *Personal Interview*, August 1984), there is now evidence that he had suggested to Carson that she make the comparison. Carson and her book were products and representatives of their time, as well as shapers of it.

Fallout, one might say, was "in the air" and it is a tribute to Carson's perceptive skill as an author that she was able to recognize and take advantage of the deep-seated cluster of social concerns surrounding it in the public's mind. Not only did she tap into this anxiety and direct it toward pesticides, she also used the public's existing understanding about the hazards of fallout to teach about the similar hazards of chemical poisons. Just as strontium 90 could travel great distances, enter the food chain, and accumulate in human tissue, so too could pesticides. Just as radioactive materials could produce chronic rather than acute poisoning, so too could pesticides. And just as exposure to radiation could produce cancer, birth defects, and mutations, so might pesticides. The public already knew the basic concepts—all it needed was a little reminding.

A distinctive feature of the contemporary environmental movement is a profound and pervasive element of fear. It is a fear that, for good or ill, colors and sometimes distorts virtually every popular analysis of major environmental problems. This is not simply a fear that we will deplete a particular natural resource, lose pristine wilderness, or be poisoned. It is the belief that we may well be facing the "end of history," that we as a species might be doomed. This anxiety burst to the surface with the destruction of Hiroshima and Nagasaki. It is rooted in the omnipresent threat of nuclear destruction.

The generation that promoted Earth Day 1970 grew up in the shadow of nuclear destruction. This threat became a tacit part of the way in which people understood their world. It is no surprise then, that the belief in the imminent end of the earth became integrated with more traditional conservation concerns. This younger generation did not create the anxiety, nor did its elder, Rachel Carson. She did, though, write one of the first and most eloquent books bridging the gap between the environmental movement and this new fearful vision of Armageddon.

4

Publication of Rachel Carson's *Silent Spring:* 1962

Carson's Original Warning About Environmental Pollutants

by Rachel Carson

Rachel Carson was a marine biologist, ecologist, and author who is considered the mother of the environmental movement. Born in 1907, Carson was reared on an expansive farm surrounded by the bounty of nature. When she went away to college, she intended to pursue her interest in writing until a course in biology shifted her focus to natural sciences. She completed a degree in zoology in 1929 at Chatham College and then earned a graduate degree in 1932 from Johns Hopkins University. In 1936 Carson went to work for the Bureau of Fisheries, where she held the dual positions of staff biologist and writer. In 1949 the bureau appointed her editor in chief.

While working for the bureau, Carson saw her first book, *Under the Sea-Wind* (1941), published. The 1940s proved difficult for Carson personally, as she struggled to tend to her aging mother and her deceased sister's two daughters. When her second book, *The Sea Around Us* was published in 1951, it attained best-seller status, thus relieving some of Carson's financial strains. The subsequent rerelease of *Under the Sea-Wind* also enjoyed best-selling status. These successes enabled her to leave her job at the bureau and concentrate on being a full-time writer. The result was 1956's *The Edge*

Rachel Carson, *Silent Spring*. New York: Houghton Mifflin, 2002. Copyright © 1990 by Roger Christie. Reproduced by permission of the publisher.

of the Sea, which was a best-seller despite lukewarm reviews.

Carson is best known, however, for her 1962 book *Silent Spring*. This book was the catalyst for the environmental movement, which is still strong today. Although readers and critics praised the book for opening the public's eyes to the dangers of pollutants, chemical companies were quick to attack the book. The erupting controversy surrounding the book brought to light certain partnerships that troubled the concerned public; the chemical industry, government agencies, and certain segments of the scientific community banded together. But the public demanded action, and a presidential advisory committee was formed to investigate the claims. This committee ultimately banned many pesticides and gave stricter guidelines for the use of others.

Carson died of cancer in 1964, but her legacy is still alive in the passion of scores of environmentalists around the globe. Although science over the years has refuted some of Carson's claims, her basic reverence for nature and ideas about humankind's responsibility to it have stood the test of time.

Town of Lush Natural Beauty

There was once a town in the heart of America where all life seemed to live in harmony with its surroundings. The town lay in the midst of a checkerboard of prosperous farms, with fields of grain and hillsides of orchards where, in spring, white clouds of bloom drifted above the green fields. In autumn, oak and maple and birch set up a blaze of color that flamed and flickered across a backdrop of pines. Then foxes barked in the hills and deer silently crossed the fields, half hidden in the mists of the fall mornings.

Along the roads, laurel, viburnum and alder, great ferns and wildflowers delighted the traveler's eye through much of the year. Even in winter the roadsides were places of beauty, where countless birds came to feed on the berries and on the seed heads of the dried weeds rising above the snow. The countryside was, in fact, famous for the abundance and variety of its bird life, and when the flood of migrants was pouring through in spring and fall people traveled from great distances to observe them. Others came to fish the streams, which flowed clear and cold out of the hills and contained shady pools where trout lay. So it had been from the days many years ago when the first settlers raised their houses, sank their wells, and built their barns.

A Wave of Destruction Strikes

Then a strange blight crept over the area and everything began to change. Some evil spell had settled on the community: mysterious maladies swept the flocks of chickens; the cattle and sheep sickened and died. Everywhere was a shadow of death. The farmers spoke of much illness among their families. In the town the doctors had become more and more puzzled by new kinds of sickness appearing among their patients. There had been several sudden and unexplained deaths, not only among adults but even among children, who would be stricken suddenly while at play and die within a few hours.

There was a strange stillness. The birds, for example—where had they gone? Many people spoke of them, puzzled and disturbed. The feeding stations in the backyards were deserted. The few birds seen anywhere were moribund; they trembled violently and could not fly. It was a spring without voices. On the mornings that had once throbbed with the dawn chorus of robins, catbirds, doves, jays, wrens, and scores of other bird voices there was now no sound; only silence lay over the fields and woods and marsh.

On the farms the hens brooded, but no chicks hatched. The farmers complained that they were unable to raise any pigs—the litters were small and the young survived only a few days. The apple trees were coming into bloom but no bees droned among the blossoms, so there was no pollination and there would be no fruit.

The roadsides, once so attractive, were now lined with browned and withered vegetation as though swept by fire. These, too, were silent, deserted by all living things. Even the streams were now lifeless. Anglers no longer visited them, for all the fish had died.

In the gutters under the eaves and between the shingles of the roofs, a white granular powder still showed a few patches; some weeks before it had fallen like snow upon the roofs and the lawns, the fields and streams.

No witchcraft, no enemy action had silenced the rebirth of new life in this stricken world. The people had done it themselves.

Metaphorical Town

This town does not actually exist, but it might easily have a thousand counterparts in America or elsewhere in the world. I know of no community that has experienced all the misfortunes I describe. Yet every one of these disasters has actually happened somewhere, and many real communities have already suffered a substantial number of them. A grim specter has crept upon us almost unnoticed, and this imagined tragedy may easily become a stark reality we all shall know.

What has already silenced the voices of spring in countless towns in America? This book is an attempt to explain.

Humankind's Power over Nature Has Become Destructive

The history of life on earth has been a history of interaction between living things and their surroundings. To a large extent, the physical form and the habits of the earth's vegetation and its animal life have been molded by the environment. Considering the whole span of earthly time, the opposite effect, in which life actually modifies its surroundings, has been relatively slight. Only within the moment of time represented by the present century has one species—man—acquired significant power to alter the nature of his world.

During the past quarter century this power has not only increased to one of disturbing magnitude but it has changed in character. The most alarming of all man's assaults upon the environment is the contamination of air, earth, rivers, and sea with dangerous and even lethal materials. This pollution is for the most part irrecoverable; the chain of evil it initiates not only in the world that must support life but in living tissues is for the most part irreversible. In this now universal contamination of the environment, chemicals are the sinister and little-recognized partners of radiation in changing the very nature of the world—the very nature of its life. Strontium 90, released through nuclear explosions into the air, comes to earth in rain or drifts down as fall-out, lodges in soil, enters into the grass or corn or wheat grown there, and in time takes up its abode in the bones of a human being, there to remain until his death. Similarly, chemicals sprayed on croplands or forests or gardens lie long in soil, entering into living organisms, passing from one to another in a chain of poisoning and death. Or they pass mysteriously by underground streams until they emerge and, through the alchemy of air and sunlight, combine into new forms that kill vegetation, sicken cattle, and work unknown harm on those who drink from once pure wells. As Albert Schweitzer [humanitarian theologian and missionary] has said, "Man can hardly even recognize the devils of his own creation."

It took hundreds of millions of years to produce the life that now inhabits the earth—eons of time in which that developing and evolving and diversifying life reached a state of adjustment and balance with its surroundings. The environment, rigorously shaping and directing the life it supported, contained elements that were hostile as well as supporting. Certain rocks gave out dangerous radiation; even within the light of the sun, from which all life draws its energy, there were short-wave radiations with power to injure. Given time—time not in years but in millennia—life adjusts, and a balance has been reached. For time is the essential ingredient; but in the modern world there is no time.

The rapidity of change and the speed with which new situations are created follow the impetuous and heedless pace of man rather than the deliberate pace of nature. Radiation is no longer merely the background radiation of rocks, the bombardment of cosmic rays, the ultraviolet of the sun that have existed before there was any life on earth; radiation is now the unnatural creation of man's tampering with the atom. The chemicals to which life is asked to make its adjustment are no longer merely the calcium and silica and copper and all the rest of the minerals washed out of the rocks and carried in rivers to the sea; they are the synthetic creations of man's inventive mind, brewed in his laboratories, and having no counterparts in nature.

To adjust to these chemicals would require time on the scale that is nature's; it would require not merely the years of a man's life but the life of generations. And even this, were it by some miracle possible, would be futile, for the new chemicals come from our laboratories in an endless stream; almost five hundred annually find their way into actual use in the United States alone. The figure is staggering and its implications are not easily grasped—500 new chemicals to which the bodies of men and animals are required somehow to adapt each year, chemicals totally outside the limits of biologic experience.

Pesticides and Insecticides Pose Major Threats

Among them are many that are used in man's war against nature. Since the mid-1940's over 200 basic chemicals have been created for use in killing insects, weeds, rodents, and other organisms described in the modern vernacular as "pests"; and they are sold under several thousand different brand names.

These sprays, dusts, and aerosols are now applied almost universally to farms, gardens, forests, and homes—nonselective chemicals that have the power to kill every insect, the "good" and the "bad," to still the song of birds and the leaping of fish in the streams, to coat the leaves with a deadly film, and to linger on in soil—all this though the intended target may be only a few weeds or insects. Can anyone believe it is possible to lay down such a barrage of poisons on the surface of the earth without making it unfit for all life? They should not be called "insecticides," but "biocides."

The whole process of spraying seems caught up in an endless spiral. Since DDT was released for civilian use, a process of escalation has been going on in which ever more toxic materials must be found. This has happened because insects, in a triumphant vindication of Darwin's principle of the survival of the fittest, have evolved super races immune to the particular insecticide used, hence a deadlier one has always to be developed—and then a deadlier one than that. It has happened also because, for reasons to be described later, destructive insects often undergo a "flareback," or resurgence, after spraying, in numbers greater than before. Thus the chemical war is never won, and all life is caught in its violent crossfire.

Along with the possibility of the extinction of mankind by nuclear war, the central problem of our age has therefore become the contamination of man's total environment with such substances of incredible potential for harm—substances that accumulate in the tissues of plants and animals and even penetrate the germ cells to shatter or alter the very material of heredity upon which the shape of the future depends.

Some would-be architects of our future look toward a time when it will be possible to alter the human germ plasm by design. But we may easily be doing so now by inadvertence, for many chemicals, like radiation, bring about gene mutations. It is ironic to think that man might determine his own future by something so seemingly trivial as the choice of an insect spray.

Insecticides Are a Greater Problem than Insects

All this has been risked—for what? Future historians may well be amazed by our distorted sense of proportion. How could intelligent beings seek to control a few unwanted species by a method that contaminated the entire environment and brought the threat of disease and death even to their own kind? Yet this is precisely what we have done. We have done it, moreover, for reasons that collapse the moment we examine them. We are told that the enormous and expanding use of pesticides is necessary to maintain farm production. Yet is our real problem not one of *overproduction?* Our farms, despite measures to remove acreages from production and to pay farmers *not* to produce, have yielded such a staggering excess of crops that the American taxpayer in 1962 is paying out more than one billion dollars a year as the total carrying cost of the surplus-food storage program. And is the situation helped when one branch of the Agriculture Department tries to reduce production while another states, as it did in 1958, "It is believed generally that reduction of crop acreages under provisions of the Soil Bank will stimulate interest in use of chemicals to obtain maximum production on the land retained in crops."

All this is not to say there is no insect problem and no need of control. I am saying, rather, that control must be geared to realities, not to mythical situations, and that the methods employed must be such that they do not destroy us along with the insects.

Modern Life Disrupts Natural Processes

The problem whose attempted solution has brought such a train of disaster in its wake is an accompaniment of our modern way of life. Long before the age of man, insects inhabited the earth— a group of extraordinarily varied and adaptable beings. Over the course of time since man's advent, a small percentage of the more than half a million species of insects have come into conflict with human welfare in two principal ways: as competitors for the food supply and as carriers of human disease.

Disease-carrying insects become important where human beings are crowded together, especially under conditions where sanitation is poor, as in time of natural disaster or war or in situations of extreme poverty and deprivation. Then control of some sort becomes necessary. It is a sobering fact, however, as we shall presently see, that the method of massive chemical control has had only limited success, and also threatens to worsen the very conditions it is intended to curb.

Under primitive agricultural conditions the farmer had few insect problems. These arose with the intensification of agriculture—the devotion of immense acreages to a single crop. Such a system set the stage for explosive increases in specific insect populations. Single-crop farming does not take advantage of the principles by which nature works; it is agriculture as an engineer might conceive it to be. Nature has introduced great variety into the landscape, but man has displayed a passion for simplifying it. Thus he undoes the built-in checks and balances by which nature holds the species within bounds. One important natural check is a limit on the amount of suitable habitat for each species. Obviously then, an insect that lives on wheat can build up its population to much higher levels on a farm devoted to wheat than on one in which wheat is intermingled with other crops to which the insect is not adapted.

The same thing happens in other situations. A generation or more ago, the towns of large areas of the United States lined their streets with the noble elm tree. Now the beauty they hopefully created is threatened with complete destruction as disease sweeps through the elms, carried by a beetle that would have only limited chance to build up large populations and to spread from tree to tree if the elms were only occasional trees in a richly diversified planting.

Insects Now Migrate to New Areas, Offsetting Balances

Another factor in the modern insect problem is one that must be viewed against a background of geologic and human history: the spreading of thousands of different kinds of organisms from their native homes to invade new territories. This worldwide migration has been studied and graphically described by the British ecologist Charles Elton in his recent book *The Ecology of Invasions.* During the Cretaceous Period, some hundred million years ago, flooding seas cut many land bridges between continents and living things found themselves confined in what Elton calls "colossal separate nature reserves." There, isolated from others of their kind, they developed many new species. When some of the land masses were joined again, about 15 million years ago, these species began to move out into new territories—a movement that is not only still in progress but is now receiving considerable assistance from man.

The importation of plants is the primary agent in the modern spread of species, for animals have almost invariably gone along with the plants, quarantine being a comparatively recent and not completely effective innovation. The United States Office of Plant Introduction alone has introduced almost 200,000 species and varieties of plants from all over the world. Nearly half of the 180 or so major insect enemies of plants in the United States are accidental imports from abroad, and most of them have come as hitchhikers on plants.

In new territory, out of reach of the restraining hand of the natural enemies that kept down its numbers in its native land, an invading plant or animal is able to become enormously abundant. Thus it is no accident that our most troublesome insects are introduced species.

Ecological Wisdom Is Largely Ignored

These invasions, both the naturally occurring and those dependent on human assistance, are likely to continue indefinitely. Quarantine and massive chemical campaigns are only extremely expensive ways of buying time. We are faced, according to Dr. Elton, "with a life-and-death need not just to find new technological means of suppressing this plant or that animal"; instead we need the basic knowledge of animal populations and their relations to their surroundings that will "promote an even balance and damp down the explosive power of outbreaks and new invasions."

Much of the necessary knowledge is now available but we do not use it. We train ecologists in our universities and even employ them in our governmental agencies but we seldom take their advice. We allow the chemical death rain to fall as though there were no alternative, whereas in fact there are many, and our ingenuity could soon discover many more if given opportunity.

We Should Not Accept a World That Compromises Nature

Have we fallen into a mesmerized state that makes us accept as inevitable that which is inferior or detrimental, as though having lost the will or the vision to demand that which is good? Such thinking, in the words of the ecologist Paul Shepard, "idealizes life with only its head out of water, inches above the limits of toleration of the corruption of its own environment . . . Why should we tolerate a diet of weak poisons, a home in insipid surroundings, a circle of acquaintances who are not quite our enemies, the noise of motors with just enough relief to prevent insanity? Who would want to live in a world which is just not quite fatal?"

Yet such a world is pressed upon us. The crusade to create a chemically sterile, insect-free world seems to have engendered a fanatic zeal on the part of many specialists and most of the so-called control agencies. On every hand there is evidence that those engaged in spraying operations exercise a ruthless power. "The regulatory entomologists . . . function as prosecutor, judge and jury, tax assessor and collector and sheriff to enforce their own orders," said Connecticut entomologist Neely Turner. The most flagrant abuses go unchecked in both state and federal agencies.

Education and Awareness to Replace Ignorance

It is not my contention that chemical insecticides must never be used. I do contend that we have put poisonous and biologically potent chemicals indiscriminately into the hands of persons largely or wholly ignorant of their potentials for harm. We have subjected enormous numbers of people to contact with these poisons, without their consent and often without their knowledge. If the Bill of Rights contains no guarantee that a citizen shall be secure against lethal poisons distributed either by private individuals or by public officials, it is surely only because our forefathers, despite their considerable wisdom and foresight, could conceive of no such problem.

I contend, furthermore, that we have allowed these chemicals to be used with little or no advance investigation of their effect on soil, water, wildlife, and man himself. Future generations are unlikely to condone our lack of prudent concern for the integrity of the natural world that supports all life.

There is still very limited awareness of the nature of the threat. This is an era of specialists, each of whom sees his own problem and is unaware of or intolerant of the larger frame into which it fits. It is also an era dominated by industry, in which the right to make a dollar at whatever cost is seldom challenged. When the public protests, confronted with some obvious evidence of damaging results of pesticide applications, it is fed little tranquilizing pills of half truth. We urgently need an end to these false assurances, to the sugar coating of unpalatable facts. It is the public that is being asked to assume the risks that the insect controllers calculate. The public must decide whether it wishes to continue on the present road, and it can do so only when in full possession of the facts. In the words of Jean Rostand, "The obligation to endure gives us the right to know."

The World Joins America in Grieving for Its Slain President

by Jim F. Heath

While riding in a Dallas motorcade, waving to people lining the streets, President John F. Kennedy was shot and killed on November 22, 1963. He was in Dallas to speak at a fund-raiser for the National Democratic Party. Although he was taken immediately to Parkland Hospital, Kennedy's wounds were too severe. He was pronounced dead at 2:00 P.M., only thirty minutes after being shot.

Americans were simultaneously bereft, outraged, and confused. The pervasive news media covered every possible aspect of the event, including theories and rumors, as it struggled to piece together what really happened. Individually and collectively, Americans felt devastated by this loss, and many found it difficult to continue with routine life. The young and popular president soon reached the status of fallen hero. Kennedy's casket was held at the Capitol so that mourners could pay their respects, and on the day of his funeral at Arlington National Cemetery, thousands of people attended the procession while 90 million viewers watched on television. Even after the capture and subsequent murder of the assassin, Lee Harvey Oswald, the American people needed to know what had happened. President Lyndon B. Johnson created the Warren Com-

Jim F. Heath, *Decade of Disillusionment: The Kennedy-Johnson Years*. Bloomington: Indiana University Press, 1975. Copyright © 1975 by Indiana University Press. Reproduced by permission.

mission to compile all the evidence on the assassination and reach factual conclusions. In 1964 the commission announced its conclusion that Oswald had been the assassin, and that there was no apparent conspiracy behind the shooting. These issues continue to fuel heated debates today.

Jim F. Heath is a history professor at Portland State University in Oregon. His other book to date is *John F. Kennedy and the Business Community* (1969). He has also contributed to *The Journal of American History.*

Kennedy Goes to Texas for Political Gain

[P resident John F.] Kennedy's preoccupation with carrying Texas [in the upcoming election] prompted him to go there in November on an openly political visit. He went hoping to unite the Democratic party in the state by welding together the two feuding factions identified with conservative Governor John Connally and liberal Senator Ralph Yarborough. His itinerary included San Antonio, Houston, Austin, Fort Worth, and Dallas, the latter in spite of scattered warnings that the ultraconservative city was rife with bitter anti-Kennedy sentiment. Only a month before a hostile crowd had spat on and jostled Adlai Stevenson when he was there for a United Nations Day speech. But on a politically oriented tour it would have raised embarrassing questions had Kennedy skipped the state's second largest city, so he scheduled a three-hour stay to include a motorcade and a luncheon speech at the impressive new Trade Mart.

Texas gave the President and his wife a rousing welcome, impressing even skeptics. Although angered by a scurrilous and tasteless advertisement in the *Dallas News* accusing him of being pro-Communist and other crimes, JFK was visibly pleased by the huge, friendly crowds that greeted him at his first three stops. Just after his plane landed at Dallas, he remarked, "This trip is turning out to be terrific. Here we are in Dallas, and it looks like everything in Texas is going to be fine for us." Minutes later, as his motorcade threaded its way slowly through the enthusiastic thousands who jammed downtown Dallas to cheer the President, Lee Harvey Oswald shot and killed John F. Kennedy with a high-powered rifle.

The President's assassination stunned not only the United

States but the entire world. Never before had the death of any individual caused such an outpouring of grief in so many far-flung spots: in Ireland, where only months before Kennedy had reaffirmed his heritage during a triumphant visit; in West Berlin, where JFK had thrilled thousands by declaring, "Today, in the world of freedom, the proudest boast is *Ich bin ein Berliner*"; in the emerging states of Africa, where Guinea's Sékou Touré declared, "I have lost my only true friend in the outside world"; in India, where people cried in the streets of New Delhi. From London, Ambassador David Bruce reported that "Great Britain has never before mourned a foreigner as it has President Kennedy." In Moscow, Premier Khrushchev hurried to the American embassy to sign the condolence book. Although there were exceptions—Red China's *Daily Worker* featured a savage cartoon entitled *"Kennedy Biting the Dust"* and Madame Nhu, widow of the late Vietnamese official, bitterly charged Kennedy with the responsibility for the murder of her husband—the global response was overwhelmingly one of sadness. Arthur Schlesinger, Jr., who recorded in memorable words the dismay and anguish of persons famous and obscure, correctly wrote, "The people of the world grieved as if they had terribly lost their own leader, friend, brother."

America Grieves Its Fallen President

In the United States a state of numbness seeped over the country. It is impossible to convey in words the gloom and agony that existed. Stunned, Americans tried to comprehend how such a crime could have occurred. It was so senseless and so unreal. Most people, whether Democrat or Republican, whether they revered or disliked the President personally, were unquestionably saddened by his death. For some, it was more than the killing of a man; it was a severe blow against the very concept of a country where public figures were free to move about, even to mingle with huge crowds, without fear of injury. Such things happened in the "banana republics" of South America but not in the United States. Yet, it had happened here.

Many businesses closed early, and so did most schools the day the President was slain. But amidst the anguish, life went strangely on. Some events planned for the weekend between the assassination and the funeral were cancelled; others continued as scheduled. The National Football League played its Sunday games to huge crowds, but television networks cancelled regular shows—and received countless complaints for doing so. Nevertheless, millions watched their sets endlessly during the long weekend, seemingly mesmerized by the endless line of mourners who passed by the President's body as it lay in state in the Capitol rotunda. Untold thousands waited in bitter weather for hours, day and night, for their brief chance to see the slain leader.

Jacqueline Kennedy, whose avid interest in the arts had helped to prime the New Frontier's emphasis on American cultural development, planned the funeral ceremony itself with an eye on historical precedent and image, but with uncommon good taste. Viewed by millions on television, it provided a needed catharsis for those who had lived in a state of shock for three days. . . .

Kennedy Becomes a Heroic Figure

The assassination contained all the ingredients of high drama: a young, handsome, popular leader cut down by violent murder in the prime of his life, leaving behind an elegantly beautiful widow, two attractive children, and a large and loyal band of mourning family and friends. Unfortunately, it also contained much of the stuff from which soap operas are made, and the post-Dallas treatment of JFK and the Kennedy family in general often seemed like a blend of serious drama and television serials. The slain President became an instant martyr, and martyrdom, as it often does, tended to confuse reality with romance. Allusions to the legendary kingdom of King Arthur and his dashing knights of the Round Table (prompted by Kennedy's publicized fondness for the musical play *Camelot*) suggested that the Kennedys and the New Frontier had brought a type of nobility to America. *"Time,"* James Reston wrote, "seems to be trying to amend to John Fitzgerald Kennedy. Robbed of his years, he is being rewarded and honored in death as he never was in life. Deprived of the place he sought in history, he has been given in compensation a place in legend."

For a year or two after his death even sober and serious students of his administration lavished praise upon Kennedy. Richard Rovere credited him with organizing "a generation of public servants who will be serving Presidents (and perhaps being Presidents) into the next century" and for "making thinking respectable in Washington. . . ." Political scientist William G. Carleton observed, "In modern times romantic heroes have become rare. Kennedy is the first in this tradition in a long time, and he is the only American in its top echelon." A year after the assassination, Reston brilliantly captured the essence of national feeling in his article, "What Was Killed Was Not Only the President But the Promise." "What was killed in Dallas was . . . the death of youth and the hope of youth, of the beauty and grace and the touch of magic. . . . He never reached his meridian: we saw him only as a rising sun."

5 John F. Kennedy Is Assassinated:
November 22, 1963

Lyndon B. Johnson Addresses Congress as the New President

by Lyndon B. Johnson

Upon the assassination of President John F. Kennedy, Vice President Lyndon B. Johnson was sworn in as the nation's new president. It was a heavy mantle, taking on the role of president to a nation caught in turmoil and grief. Johnson faced the task of honoring Kennedy's legacy and vision for the nation while also shaping his own presidency. Luckily, Johnson was a tough man with a no-nonsense Texas style that the American people soon accepted.

Born in 1908, Johnson came from a family with deep roots in the American West. His ancestors were among the settlers who set out to tame the West, and others were major players in Texas's war for independence. When his father entered the Texas legislature in 1917, Johnson got his first glimpses into the world of politics. He found it endlessly fascinating. After high school he worked a series of odd jobs before attending Southwest Texas State University and becoming a teacher. His passion for politics, however, eventually took him to the nation's capital. In 1931 Johnson went to work in Washington, D.C., as a congressional secretary.

In 1934 he married Claudia Alta Taylor, already known as "Lady Bird." Her refined presence often proved an invaluable counterpoint

---

Lyndon B. Johnson, address to a joint session of the United States Congress, Washington, DC, November 27, 1963.

to Johnson's rough, outspoken nature. Through the 1930s and 1940s, Johnson held various political positions, gradually working his way up to a Senate seat in 1948. He gained power in the Senate, and in 1960 Kennedy asked him to be his presidential running mate.

Johnson was an energetic and involved vice president whose particular interests were space exploration and civil rights. When Kennedy was assassinated, Johnson became the president within hours. Despite his pain that Kennedy's assassination had taken place in his beloved home state, Johnson did his best to separate his emotions from the task at hand. The country needed leadership and reassurance, and it looked to Johnson to provide it.

In the following speech Johnson addresses Congress for the first time as president. The tone is reverent but confident and determined. Johnson's leadership apparently met the expectations of Americans, as he won his 1964 bid for reelection.

The PRESIDENT. Mr. Speaker, Mr. President, Members of the House, Members of the Senate, my fellow Americans, all I have I would have given gladly not to be standing here today.

The greatest leader of our time has been struck down by the foulest deed of our time. Today John Fitzgerald Kennedy lives on in the immortal words and works that he left behind. He lives on in the mind and memories of mankind. He lives on in the hearts of his countrymen.

No words are sad enough to express our sense of loss. No words are strong enough to express our determination to continue the forward thrust of America that he began. [Applause.]

President Kennedy's Vision Is His Legacy

The dream of conquering the vastness of space—the dream of partnership across the Atlantic, and across the Pacific as well—the dream of a Peace Corps in less developed nations—the dream of education for all of our children—the dream of jobs for all who seek them and need them—the dream of care for our elderly—the dream of an all-out attack on mental illness—and above all, the dream of equal rights for all Americans, whatever their race or color [applause]—these and other American dreams have been vitalized by his drive and by his dedication.

Now the ideas and the ideals which he so nobly represented must and will be translated into effective action. [Applause.]

Under John Kennedy's leadership, this Nation has demonstrated that it has the courage to seek peace, and it has the fortitude to risk war. We have proved that we are a good and reliable friend to those who seek peace and freedom. We have shown that we can also be a formidable foe to those who reject the path of peace and those who seek to impose upon us or our allies the yoke of tyranny.

America Will Remain Strong in International Affairs

This Nation will keep its commitments from South Vietnam to West Berlin. [Applause.] We will be unceasing in the search for peace; resourceful in our pursuit of areas of agreement, even with those with whom we differ—and generous and loyal to those who join with us in common cause.

In this age when there can be no losers in peace and no victors in war, we must recognize the obligation to match national strength with national restraint. [Applause.] We must be prepared at one and the same time for both the confrontation of power and the limitation of power. We must be ready to defend the national interest and to negotiate the common interest. This is the path that we shall continue to pursue. Those who test our courage will find it strong and those who seek our friendship will find it honorable. We will demonstrate anew that the strong can be just in the use of strength—and the just can be strong in the defense of justice. And let all know we will extend no special privilege and impose no persecution.

America Will Remain Committed to Its Citizens

We will carry on the fight against poverty and misery, ignorance and disease—in other lands and in our own.

We will serve all of the Nation, not one section or one sector, or one group, but all Americans. [Applause.] These are the United States—a united people with a united purpose.

Our American unity does not depend upon unanimity. We have differences; but now, as in the past, we can derive from those differences strength, not weakness, wisdom, not despair. Both as a people and as a Government we can unite upon a program, a program which is wise, just, enlightened, and constructive.

For thirty-two years, Capitol Hill has been my home. I have shared many moments of pride with you—pride in the ability of the Congress of the United States to act; to meet any crisis; to distill from our differences strong programs of national action.

President Johnson's Commitment to the People

An assassin's bullet has thrust upon me the awesome burden of the Presidency. I am here today to say I need your help, I cannot bear this burden alone. I need the help of all Americans in all America. [Applause.] This Nation has experienced a profound shock and in this critical moment it is our duty—yours and mine—as the Government of the United States—to do away with uncertainty and doubt and delay and to show that we are capable of decisive action [applause]—that from the brutal loss of our leader we will derive not weakness but strength—that we can and will act and act now.

From this Chamber of representative government let all the world know, and none misunderstand, that I rededicate this Government to the unswerving support of the United Nations [applause]—to the honorable and determined execution of our commitments to our allies [applause]—to the maintenance of military strength second to none—to the defense of the strength and stability of the dollar [applause]—to the expansion of our foreign trade [applause]—to the reinforcement of our programs of mutual assistance and cooperation in Asia and Africa [applause]— and to our Alliance for Progress in this hemisphere. [Applause.]

On the 20th day of January, in 1961, John F. Kennedy told his countrymen that our national work would not be finished "in the first thousand days, nor in the life of this administration, nor even perhaps in our lifetime on this planet. But"—he said—"let us begin."

Today in this moment of new resolve, I would say to my fellow Americans, let us continue. [Applause.]

Honor Kennedy's Memory by Passing His Legislation

This is our challenge—not to hesitate, not to pause, not to turn about and linger over this evil moment but to continue on our course so that we may fulfill the destiny that history has set for us. Our most immediate tasks are here on this Hill.

First, no memorial oration or eulogy could more eloquently honor President Kennedy's memory than the earliest possible passage of the civil rights bill for which he fought so long. [Applause.] We have talked long enough in this country about equal rights. We have talked for 100 years or more. It is time now to write the next chapter—and to write it in the books of law. [Applause.]

I urge you again, as I did in 1957, and again in 1960, to enact a civil rights law so that we can move forward to eliminate from this Nation every trace of discrimination and oppression that is based upon race or color. [Applause.] There could be no greater source of strength to this Nation both at home and abroad.

And second, no act of ours could more fittingly continue the work of President Kennedy than the early passage of the tax bill for which he fought all this long year. [Applause.] This is a bill designed to increase our national income and Federal revenues, and to provide insurance against recession. That bill, if passed without delay, means more security for those now working, more jobs for those now without them, and more incentive for our economy.

Lyndon B. Johnson was a strong advocate for civil rights. He is pictured above, signing the Civil Rights Bill of 1968.

Adopt a Spirit of Action

In short, this is no time for delay. It is time for action [applause]—strong, forward-looking action on the pending education bills to help bring the light of learning to every home and hamlet in America, strong, forward-looking action on youth employment opportunities, strong, forward-looking action on the pending foreign aid bill, making clear that we are not forfeiting our responsibilities to this hemisphere or to the world, nor erasing executive flexibility in the conduct of our foreign affairs [applause]—and strong, prompt, and forward-looking action on the remaining appropriation bills. [Applause.]

In this new spirit of action the Congress can expect the full cooperation and support of the executive branch. And in particular I pledge that the expenditures of your Government will be administered with the utmost thrift and frugality. [Applause.] I ask your help. I will insist that the Government get a dollar's value for a dollar spent. The Government will set an example of prudence and economy. [Applause.] This does not mean that we will not meet our unfilled needs or that we will not honor our commitments. We will do both.

As one who has long served in both Houses of the Congress, I firmly believe in the independence and the integrity of the legislative branch. [Applause.] I promise you that I shall always respect this. It is deep in the marrow of my bones.

With equal firmness, I believe in the capacity and I believe in the ability of the Congress, despite the divisions of opinion which characterize our Nation, to act—to act wisely, to act vigorously, to act speedily when the need arises.

The need is here. The need is now.

Hope for a Harmonious America

We meet in grief; but let us also meet in renewed dedication and renewed vigor. Let us meet in action, in tolerance and in mutual understanding.

John Kennedy's death commands what his life conveyed—that America must move forward. [Applause.] The time has come for Americans of all races and creeds and political beliefs to understand and to respect one another. [Applause.] So let us put an end to the teaching and preaching of hate and evil and violence. [Applause.] Let us turn away from the fanatics of the far left and the far right, from the apostles of bitterness and bigotry, from those defiant of law, and those who pour venom into our Nation's bloodstream. [Applause.]

I profoundly hope that the tragedy and the torment of these terrible days will bind us together in new fellowship, making us one people in our hour of sorrow. So let us here highly resolve that John Fitzgerald Kennedy did not live—or die—in vain. [Applause.] And on this Thanksgiving eve, as we gather together to ask the Lord's blessing, and give Him our thanks, let us unite in those familiar and cherished words:

America, America, God shed His grace on thee, And crown thy good With brotherhood From sea to shining sea.

The Performance That Changed Popular Music Forever

by Jeff Guinn

Nobody could have anticipated the profound impact the Beatles would have on rock-and-roll music. With a major following in Great Britain and Europe, the Beatles made their way to the United States. Thanks to a major promotional effort by Capitol Records, the Beatles began the charge of the "British invasion" on February 9, 1964, when they first appeared on *The Ed Sullivan Show*. Sullivan's show was a popular variety show that featured established acts and new performers Sullivan favored. By the time the Beatles landed at Kennedy International Airport in New York City to appear on Sullivan's show, thousands of screaming fans were waiting. On the night of the performance, an estimated 73 million viewers watched. Beatlemania was in full force, and the boys had just arrived.

The following article was written in commemoration of the thirtieth anniversary of this historic appearance. Jeff Guinn relates the lesser known details of the Beatles's booking on *The Ed Sullivan Show* and the history that was made that night. He also describes the unprecedented enthusiasm of the fans at every stop on the Beatles's first American tour.

Jeff Guinn is a staff writer for the *Fort Worth Star-Telegram*. His writings also include *Our Land Before We Die: The Proud Story of the Seminole Negro* (2002) and the afterword of *Fast Copy* (2001).

America Welcomes the Beatles

After just three decades, legend already has it that on Feb. 9, 1964, a Sunday night, the Beatles were introduced to America on CBS' *The Ed Sullivan Show*, and neither popular music nor the very fabric of society has been the same since.

There's been much pondering on why the Beatles were so instantly immense, with general agreement that the attraction of their unique coiffures and sound mingled favorably with an American psyche still reeling from the assassination of President John F. Kennedy a scant eleven weeks earlier. Hair and harmonies collided with horror and made history.

How the Beatles Were Booked on *The Ed Sullivan Show*

True, but like most legends, only partially so. How Sullivan became aware of the Beatles, and why the band was able to get his attention at a London airport four months before their first appearance on his show, is really due to a Beatles performance on *another* television program, British TV's *Sunday Night at the London Palladium*.

Before Sunday night, Oct. 13, 1963, the Beatles were stars of the British pop scene, but no more so than crooners Tommy Steele, Cliff Richard and Matt Munro. The band had signed its first recording contract with Parlophone, the English branch of Capitol Records, 14 months earlier. They'd already been turned down by several other labels, each better established in Britain's so-called "rock 'n' roll" market.

Love Me Do, the Beatles' first British single, was released on Oct. 4, 1962. Though the band's manager, Brian Epstein, bought 10,000 copies, the record barely cracked England's Top 20 charts, peaking at No. 17.

But in January 1963 the band's second British single, *Please Please Me*, became a No. 1 hit, as did its follow-up *From Me to You* in April. August 1963 marked the English release of *She Loves You*, and that third consecutive No. 1 elevated the Beatles to approximately the same national status as Richard, who'd had five No. 1's in a row.

In recognition, the Beatles were invited to appear on BBC-TV's *Palladium* broadcast. This was of immense significance; *Palladium* was to Britain what *Sullivan* was to America, a Sunday night primetime broadcast watched by almost everyone, and, by virtue of its status, the most sought-after booking for any British entertainers. If you appeared on *Palladium*, you'd made it. The Beatles and Epstein were thrilled.

What happened on the broadcast was expected; the Beatles performed five songs and were received enthusiastically by the studio audience. Events before and after the show got all the headlines in Monday's British papers. A mob of teenage girls, variously estimated by the press to have numbered between 50 and 500, tried to break into the Palladium to see their heroes in concert and, afterward, mobbed their getaway car.

It was later suggested by Beatles insiders that Epstein may have hired the girls to show up and scream. Certainly there weren't as many as reported; one nonjournalist witness counted just eight.

In any event, the Beatles had conquered Britain. Thanks to an incident at Heathrow airport, America was next.

By late 1963, *The Ed Sullivan Show* had been a staple of U.S. show business for more than a decade. Its dumpy host, a former newspaper entertainment columnist, ruled his program with an iron hand. Sullivan liked to discover unknown performers and turn them into stars. On Oct. 31, 1963, he landed in London to begin a brief visit of England and Europe in hopes of scouting acts good enough to merit the honor of appearing on his program. Sullivan was especially interested in the ability of foreign acts to gain strong popularity in their native countries.

And on Oct. 31, Sullivan was informed that his outbound flight was delayed because teen-age girls were mobbing the airport to welcome back a pop group named the Beatles whose members were returning from a short concert tour in Sweden.

One week later, Epstein flew to New York to negotiate an appearance by the Beatles on Sullivan's show.

Beatles Manager Brian Epstein Had His Eye on the American Market

It wasn't Epstein's first attempt to sell his band in the States. A year earlier, he and George Martin, who produced the Beatles' music for Parlophone, had tried to convince Capitol Records to release *Please Please Me* in America. Label executive Jay Livingstone, to his eternal disgrace, replied, "We don't think the Beatles will do anything in this market."

Rebuffed, Epstein and Martin eventually struck a deal for *Please Please Me* on Vee Jay Records, a small Chicago label. Released in America in February 1963, the record bombed. *From Me To You* was also turned down by Capitol and issued by Vee Jay; it managed to reach No. 116 in the singles charts. *She Loves You*, issued in August by Swan Records after yet another Capitol rejection, didn't even do that well.

So Sullivan's good impression at Heathrow Airport was tempered by the Beatles' apparent inability to impress music fans in the United States. He eventually offered Epstein a take-it-or-leave-it deal: Though most acts on Sullivan's show received a flat $7,500 per appearance, he'd pay the Beatles a total of $10,000 for three performances—live appearances on Feb. 9 and 16, plus a third, taped performance Feb. 23. Epstein agreed to take the minimal fee in exchange for top billing on the Feb. 9 show. (Mitzi Gaynor headlined on Feb. 16.)

Capitol Records Promotes the Band in America

Based on the upcoming *Sullivan Show* appearance, Capitol agreed to handle the Jan. 13, 1964, U.S. release of the Beatles' latest single, *I Want to Hold Your Hand*. A few American disc jockeys somehow got hold of the British version of the song, which had been issued Nov. 29. The subsequent unscheduled air play stirred enough listener interest for Capitol to press one million copies instead of the scheduled 200,000, and move its release date up to Dec. 26. With the help of a major label's big budget promotional efforts, *I Want to Hold Your Hand* was No. 1 in the United States three weeks later. The Beatles would arrive in America with a hit single.

Arrival in America

On Feb. 7, teen-age British girls mobbed Heathrow Airport to see the Beatles off and teen-age American girls did the same at Kennedy to welcome them to the United States. The objects of their affection spent a nervous flight reminiscing about fellow British pop star Cliff Richard's inability to crack the American market. Several British newspapers had reporters along on the

The Beatles wave to thousands of screaming fans after their arrival at Kennedy International Airport in New York City.

flight; McCartney made his "what do [Americans] want with us" comment to the aptly named journalist George Harrison, who wrote for the Liverpool *Echo*.

Paul, along with John, George and Ringo, was amazed to be greeted by a pack of screaming fans. The Kennedy mob scene was at least in part the work of Nicky Byrne, an American hustler who'd gotten permission from Epstein to develop and market Beatles products in the United States. Before the band's arrival, Byrne got disc jockeys on popular New York radio stations to tell listeners there'd be free Beatles T-shirts for everyone who turned out to greet them at the airport. (Byrne got rich off the Beatles; Epstein, inept at most business dealings, agreed to give Byrne ninety percent of all U.S. profits from "authorized" Beatles lunch boxes, fake wigs, dolls and the like, with just ten percent going to the band and Epstein. In fact, most celebrities then and now get the bulk of profits from such endorsed products.)

The Beatles checked into the Plaza Hotel just off New York's Central Park, and chaos instantly ensued. Radio personality Murray the K sneaked in, bringing along a crew to send out live interviews. Several U.S. pop stars, including the Ronettes, came to call. George Harrison (the musician) came down with the flu.

Preparation for the Live Show

The next day, three Beatles rehearsed for Sullivan's show. George was too sick to participate, and Sullivan joked that, if necessary, he'd put on a wig and join the band himself rather than cancel their appearance and waste such widespread, free publicity.

Sunday dawned; the Beatles slept late into the afternoon, then reported to the Sullivan set in a downtown New York theater. George was well enough to go on after all.

Just before the live broadcast, Epstein approached Sullivan, who was understandably nervous. Even in pre-cable television, it was anticipated an amazing eighty percent of all American TVs would be tuned in. If the Beatles flopped, Sullivan might be an overnight laughingstock.

"I would like to know the exact wording of your introduction," Epstein requested in his veddy British tone.

"I would like you to get lost," Sullivan replied in his nasty Noo Yawk snarl.

Magic followed. Sullivan opened the show with a few comments about "unprecedented excitement" and then introduced the Beatles, painfully enunciating the "t." Curtains opened and there they were, standing in the middle of a set with giant white arrows pointing to them.

McCartney counted off "One, two, three" and the band launched into *All My Loving* while the studio audience, cannily packed by Sullivan with teen-age girls, screamed wildly. It was no accident that a McCartney tune was featured first. Epstein thought it better for American audiences to be greeted by the bass player's cuteness rather than Lennon's rougher-edged persona.

When *All My Loving* concluded 100 seconds later, the Beatles followed with a McCartney-sung show tune, *'Til There Was You* from *The Music Man* rather than another of their own compositions.

She Loves You concluded the Beatles' first set; studio lettering superimposed each of their names onscreen during the song. Along with Lennon's name came the admonition, "Sorry, girls, he's married."

On the second half of the show, Sullivan prefaced his introduction by informing the nation that Elvis Presley and his manager, Tom Parker, had just sent a wire wishing the Beatles great U.S. success. Then the group played *I Saw Her Standing There* and *I Want to Hold Your Hand.* Afterward, they shook Sullivan's hand and stood beside him, smiling into living rooms all over America. Beatlemania was official in the United States, endorsed by a stunned New York Police Department with the announcement Feb. 10 that, during the Beatles' performances the night before, *not one* hubcap had been stolen in New York City and its outlying boroughs.

The Beatles Continue a Brief Tour in the United States

The Beatles stayed in the States for eight more days. They performed concerts in Washington, D.C., and in New York's Carnegie Hall (where they were originally booked as a "string quartet" because staff of the venerable venue had never allowed a pop group on its hallowed stage) before arriving in Miami Beach to make their second appearance on Sullivan's show. (Occasionally it was broadcast from places other than New York.)

This time, the first Beatle set included *She Loves You, This Boy* and *All My Loving*, with *I Saw Her Standing There, From Me to You* and *I Want to Hold Your Hand* performed in the second half of the show. Again, only Paul got a solo turn; otherwise, he and John shared lead vocals. It wasn't until the taped Beatles segment on Sullivan's Feb. 23 show that, with *Twist and Shout*, John Lennon had the chance to sing solo lead to American TV audiences.

Now, just over thirteen years since John Lennon was murdered, comes news that the surviving three Beatles may work together again as part of a multipart British TV documentary on the band. Most true fans cringe at the thought; what new music could ever equal the old? [Note: As of the publication of this anthology, John Lennon has been gone twenty-two years, and George Harrison has been gone for two years.]

For most Americans, though, the Beatles' Feb. 9, 1964, appearance on *The Ed Sullivan Show* will always remain their initial exposure to the band. And, as all of us who are old enough to look back on it realize, there are no happier memories than those of first love.

7 Martin Luther King Jr. Is Assassinated: April 4, 1968

King's Assassination Is an American Tragedy

by Robert F. Kennedy

In the wake of Martin Luther King Jr.'s assassination, the voice of Robert F. Kennedy was one that people would hear. A tireless advocate of civil rights and an ardent supporter and admirer of King, Kennedy understood the rage and devastation felt by King's followers.

Kennedy was born in 1925 in Brookline, Massachusetts, to what would become an American political dynasty. His older brother, John, enjoyed a fruitful political career with Robert's help in campaigning. When John, who was president in 1963, was assassinated, Robert suffered deeply. As the turbulent 1960s proceeded, Robert pursued his own political career, having had the experience of being the attorney general during his brother's presidency. He held strong positions for civil rights, opportunities for minorities, and improved conditions for the poor, so he and King became friends and allies. On March 31, 1963, Kennedy announced his candidacy for the presidency. Five days later he was shocked and saddened to hear that King had been gunned down outside his motel in Memphis. Before the day was over, Kennedy addressed a

Robert F. Kennedy, speech, Indianapolis, Indiana, April 4, 1968.

group of King's grieving admirers in an effort to encourage and guide them. Kennedy himself was assassinated on June 6 of the same year.

I have bad news for you, for all of our fellow citizens, and people who love peace all over the world, and that is that Martin Luther King was shot and killed tonight. Martin Luther King dedicated his life to love and to justice for his fellow human beings, and he died because of that effort.

In this difficult day, in this difficult time for the United States, it is perhaps well to ask what kind of a nation we are and what direction we want to move in. For those of you who are black—considering the evidence there evidently is that there were white people who were responsible—you can be filled with bitterness, with hatred, and a desire for revenge. We can move in that direction as a country, in great polarization—black people amongst black; white people amongst white, filled with hatred toward one another.

Or we can make an effort, as Martin Luther King did, to understand and to comprehend, and to replace that violence, that stain of bloodshed that has spread across our land, with an effort to understand with compassion and love.

For those of you who are black and are tempted to be filled with hatred and distrust at the injustice of such an act, against all white people, I can only say that I feel in my own heart the same kind of feeling. I had a member of my family killed, but he was killed by a white man. But we have to make an effort in the United States, we have to make an effort to understand, to go beyond these rather difficult times.

Seek Wisdom and Compassion, Not Revenge

My favorite poet was Aeschylus. He wrote: "In our sleep, pain which cannot forget falls drop by drop upon the heart until, in our own despair, against our will, comes wisdom through the awful grace of God."

What we need in the United States is not division; what we need in the United States is not hatred; what we need in the United States is not violence or lawlessness; but love and wisdom, and compassion toward one another, and a feeling of jus-

Martin Luther King Jr., a tireless advocate of civil rights, was gunned down outside his motel in Memphis in 1963.

tice toward those who still suffer within our country, whether they be white or they be black.

So I shall ask you tonight to return home, to say a prayer for the family of Martin Luther King, that's true, but more importantly to say a prayer for our own country, which all of us love— a prayer for understanding and that compassion of which I spoke.

We can do well in this country. We will have difficult times; we've had difficult times in the past; we will have difficult times in the future. It is not the end of violence; it is not the end of lawlessness; it is not the end of disorder.

But the vast majority of white people and the vast majority of black people in this country want to live together, want to improve the quality of our life, and want justice for all human beings who abide in our land.

Let us dedicate ourselves to what the Greeks wrote so many years ago: to tame the savageness of man and make gentle the life of this world.

Let us dedicate ourselves to that, and say a prayer for our country and for our people.

The Moon Landing and Its Importance to Politics, Science, Technology, Economics, and Morale

by Alan J. Levine

When the lunar module *Eagle* landed on the Moon's surface on July 20, 1969, it was the first time in history that people landed in outer space. Although numerous missions had been completed in which astronauts entered space, and two American missions had even neared the Moon, this mission was the first one in which a human foot was placed on any surface but Earth's. It was monumental.

The Apollo spacecraft that would take Neil Armstrong, Edwin Aldrin Jr., and Michael Collins to the Moon was launched from Florida's Cape Kennedy (now Cape Canaveral) on July 16 as half a million onlookers cheered. Only eight years earlier, President John F. Kennedy had set his sights on getting an American to the Moon.

Alan J. Levine, "To the Moon," *The Missile and Space Race*. Westport, CT: Praeger Publishers, 1994. Copyright © 1994 by Alan J. Levine. Reproduced by permission of Greenwood Publishing Group, Inc., Westport, CT.

During the 1960s the space race between the United States and the Soviet Union was competitive and carried with it the assumption of technological superiority. To get to the Moon first, then, was a Cold War victory. As the three astronauts made their way to the Moon, they kept in contact with the NASA space station in Houston. They also gave television audiences the rare thrill of seeing life in space as they used cameras to show their daily routine, along with stunning views of Earth from the windows of their cabin. On Sunday, July 20, Armstrong and Aldrin entered *Eagle* while Collins manned *Columbia*. As Armstrong stepped onto the Moon's surface and then the two astronauts walked on the Moon and planted the America flag, half a billion people watched on television. The event was important historically, scientifically, politically, and symbolically.

Alan J. Levine is an author and historian who specializes in international affairs, especially with regard to Russia. In addition to numerous articles about the Cold War, he has written many books, including *The Soviet Union, the Communist Movement, and the World: Prelude to the Cold War* (1990) and *The Missile and Space Race* (1994).

T he crew that would land on the moon consisted entirely of veterans of Gemini [a two-person spacecraft used for training and research]. The civilian commander, Neil Armstrong, a Korean War Navy pilot, had flown the X-15 as well. LM [Lunar Module] pilot Buzz Aldrin and Command Module pilot Michael Collins were West Pointers and USAF [U.S. Air Force] professionals. All were capable, and Armstrong and Aldrin were commonly regarded as the smartest men in the astronaut corps. Although Aldrin had personal problems that would surface after his return (and that he would overcome), none of that was apparent on the trip. The crew had trained to the nth degree; every move they would make had been rehearsed carefully.

On July 16, 1969, they had a smooth liftoff from earth, beginning the most closely watched event in history. On their second orbit around the earth, the S-IVB [*Saturn* IV rocket] fired again; after a rough ride of six minutes, they reached escape velocity. The flight out was comfortable, none were spacesick. Only one mid-course correction was needed. Going into orbit around the moon, they carefully checked their equipment and then rested for nine hours. On the morning of July 20, Armstrong and Aldrin crawled from Command Module *Columbia* to Lunar Module *Eagle*. They undocked and tested the thrusters and all vital systems. At precisely the right moment, Armstrong fired the descent engine. It took twelve minutes to reach the surface; nothing actually went wrong, but alarms caused by computer overloads were irritating. At a height of just over 2,000 feet, Armstrong saw that they were coming down next to a rocky crater in an area strewn with boulders. He made a last-minute lateral adjustment to reach a smooth surface a few hundred feet away. At 4:17 P.M. Eastern Standard Time, *Eagle* landed on a level plain that was covered with many small craters and ridges, in the east central part of the Sea of Tranquility (Mare Tranquillatis) just north of the moon's equator and just off the center of the moon's nearside. *Eagle* had twenty seconds of fuel left. Characteristically, Armstrong was not quite satisfied with his performance, but few others would quarrel with it. The first humans had reached another world.

Unknown to the men aboard *Eagle* or a watching world, those monitoring the craft on earth were very worried. Pressure sensors indicated that something was blocking a fuel line; they believed it was a bit of frozen fuel and feared that heat from the engine would make it explode. Some at Grumman urged telling *Eagle* to take off immediately, but *Columbia* was not then in a position for the two to rendezvous. Some favored "burping" the engine, but nothing was done about the problem, and whatever it was vanished of its own accord.

Armstrong and Aldrin Set Foot on the Moon's Surface

Armstrong and Aldrin were supposed to take a long rest before leaving *Eagle*, but they were in no mood to wait. It took several hours to get ready to emerge. At 10:39 P.M., Armstrong clambered down to the surface, declaring that it was "one small step for [a] man, one giant leap for mankind." (Much to his irritation, he swallowed the *a* or the microphone failed to pick it up.) On the way down, he had deployed a TV camera. He examined the surface and quickly scooped up a sample in case they had to leave early. Then Aldrin emerged, pronouncing the scene one of "magnificent desolation." After examining *Eagle* for any damage, they practiced walking in low gravity. Armstrong moved the TV camera away from the LM, and Aldrin began setting up the relatively few but valuable experiments they had brought. NASA's directors had decided to make few demands on this first, relatively brief visit; the instrument package originally planned had been cut down in the face of the growing weight of the LM and to provide a greater margin of safety. Aldrin erected a solar wind sample collector. They then planted the Stars and Stripes, discovering that the ground under the surface was fairly hard. This exercise, which seems rather pointless since the United States had no intention of claiming the moon, was followed by a call from President Nixon, continuing a dubious tradition initiated by Kennedy. On the whole, however, the patriotic waste of time was kept to a minimum. The astronauts then emplaced a passive seismic experiment—four seismometers that would remain on the moon to report to earth, and a laser mirror reflector (which would enable more precise measurements of the distance between the earth and the moon, fluctuations in the earth's rotation, and the movements of the crust involved in the still controversial continental drift theory). They took many photographs and samples of rock. Fortunately, Armstrong had been the best

Astronauts Neil Armstrong, Michael Collins, and Edwin Aldrin Jr. are welcomed to New York City after their historic flight to the moon.

student of geology among the nonscientists in the astronaut corps, and he made effective use of the limited time.

The Return Home with Materials and Data

The controllers on earth extended the planned outing by a quarter of an hour; the crew finally returned to *Eagle* with 50 pounds of rocks and the solar wind collector. They had been outside only about two hours. After a fitful sleep, they departed at 1:54 P.M. on July 21. Four hours later, they rendezvoused with *Columbia.* The men transferred their gear and specimens, jettisoned *Eagle*, and had an easy flight home, landing in the Pacific on July 24. The sequel to the great journey was a tedious twenty-one days in quarantine, joined by a few technicians possibly contaminated by contact with lunar materials. The precautions were of dubious value, since much soil had been tracked into the LM and then the *Columbia*, and was released into the air and sea when *Columbia*'s hatch was opened. The recovery crew, at least, would have been contaminated but was not quarantined. No one had really expected life on the moon, and it was even less likely that if there were any organisms there they could harm terrestrials.

There was nothing to worry about. No evidence of life, and almost no organic materials, were found in the samples. They proved to be igneous rocks, not quite like their earth counterparts. They showed that the moon's composition was in fact different, although not grossly so, from earth's and proved that the moon had been at least partly molten and had once had a magnetic field. This knocked out the old idea that the moon might have fissioned from earth; it had formed separately. . . .

Scientific and Technological Benefits

The information gained by the Apollo expeditions and supplemented by the Soviet unmanned effort enabled the formation of a rough picture of the moon's structure, composition, and history. It became fairly clear that it had never had any life, and probably no free water either. But it was a differentiated body that had undergone some changes early in its history. All rocks found were igneous; none were sedimentary or metamorphic. Under a loose layer of rubble, a crust (largely of anorthosite and thicker on the far side than the near side) went down an average of 37 miles; below that there was a mantle some 625 miles deep, and, probably, a partly molten core of silicates or iron. The moon had once had a magnetic field, which had largely disappeared. The minerals in the crust contained few volatiles but a higher percentage of radioactives than the cosmic average. The moon's composition differed considerably from the earth and might well have formed in a different part of the solar system before being captured by the earth. It might never have been completely molten, but its outer layer had melted early in its history and probably had remelted in parts later. The vast basins, called seas, had been gouged out by cosmic impacts 3.9 to 4.1 billion years before; the highlands retained the oldest rocks on the moon— over four billion years old. The craters proved overwhelmingly meteoritic in origin. There had been volcanic activity, but the moon had long been dead geologically. Its crust was not rich in valuable minerals (with the vital exception, perhaps, of helium-3, deposited by the solar wind and almost unavailable on earth, which might be the best fuel for future nuclear fusion reactors). But there were ample materials for building permanent bases and, perhaps, schemes of space industrialization. Whatever its other consequences and original purpose, Apollo's true value may have been as the costliest prospecting job in history. The Soviet probes were a great achievement, but no unmanned effort could have duplicated Apollo's samples; without the larger rocks it brought back, the soil the unmanned probes retrieved would have been downright misleading.

Apart from the scientific data gained and speculative long-range gains, the Apollo program had short-term side-effects and technological gains, or spinoffs, which were a significant recompense for the $25 billion expended. (The space program as a whole, including Apollo, undoubtedly paid for itself just through improved weather reporting. It was estimated that by 1971 NASA's weather and earth resources satellites alone were saving $3 billion a year, and perhaps tens of thousands of lives, by tracking storms, plant diseases, and forest fires from orbit. Of course, that sort of activity could have been carried on without Apollo, or indeed any manned flights.) Although sometimes exaggerated (for example, the useful plastic teflon, actually a product of the Manhattan Project, was sometimes hijacked by ardent advocates of Apollo), many useful techniques and products were developed. Building the Saturns involved many advances in industrial technology, especially the development of new aluminum alloys and welding techniques, new tools such as the "electromagnetic hammer," new forms of insulation, and techniques to make and store cryogenic fluids on a large scale. The project's investment in electronics, especially biomedical devices and computers, was particularly productive. It contributed to the development of CAT scanners, heart-monitoring devices and other biosensors, and portable kidney machines. And Apollo generated jobs. Charles Murray, who studied both Apollo and the social programs of the era, concluded that Apollo produced as many jobs as Johnson's whole Great Society program.

Armstrong and Aldrin Describe the Moon Landing

by Neil Armstrong and Edwin Aldrin Jr.

Although they had loved the idea of flying since childhood, astronauts Neil Armstrong and Edwin "Buzz" Aldrin Jr. could never have imagined that they would make history as the first men to walk on the Moon. After extensive preparation, the mission launched on July 16, 1969. Aboard the spacecraft were parts of the Wright brothers' plane that had successfully flown at Kitty Hawk in 1903, a tribute to the American dream of flight. On July 20 Armstrong and Aldrin touched down on the Moon, ensuring forever their places in history.

Armstrong was born on August 5, 1930, in Wapakoneta, Ohio. He took an early interest in flying, doing odd jobs to earn money for flying lessons. He earned his wings at the age of sixteen. After high school he studied aeronautical engineering on a navy scholarship and served in active duty during the Korean War. He completed seventy-eight combat missions and won three medals. He then became a research flight pilot before his selection by the National Aeronautics and Space Administration (NASA) to be an astronaut. A capable commander of space missions, Armstrong was selected for *Apollo 11*, which would go to the Moon. After his historic flight to the Moon, Armstrong worked as deputy associate administrator of aeronautics for NASA. In 1971 he joined the University of Cincinnati as a professor of aerospace engineering. Eight years later he started his own computer systems company while acting as an adviser to the space program.

Neil Armstrong and Edwin Aldrin Jr., "Voice from Moon: The Eagle Has Landed," *New York Times*, July 21, 1969.

Aldrin was born on January 20, 1930, in Montclair, New Jersey. He came from a military family and graduated third in his class at West Point in 1951. As an air force officer, he fought in the Korean War, where he earned the Distinguished Flying Cross. After the war he worked as an air force instructor, academy aide, flight instructor, and then flight commander for a squadron in Germany. In 1959 he became interested in the growing space program, so he completed a doctorate degree at the Massachusetts Institute of Technology in 1963. Later that year NASA selected him for its astronaut program. He proved himself a resourceful and competent astronaut and was chosen for *Apollo 11*. After the mission, Aldrin became commander of the test pilot school at Edwards Air Force Base. Dissatisfied, he resigned in 1971. Although celebrities rarely discussed addictions, Aldrin publicly admitted his struggle to recover from alcoholism and depression. In 1972 he started his own spacecraft company, Starcraft Enterprises. He wrote his autobiography in 1974 and collaborated on science fiction books in 1996 and 2000.

E AGLE (the lunar module): Houston, Tranquility Base here. The Eagle has landed.

HOUSTON: Roger, Tranquility, we copy you on the ground. You've got a bunch of guys about to turn blue. We're breathing again. Thanks a lot.

TRANQUILITY BASE: Thank you.

HOUSTON: You're looking good here.

TRANQUILITY BASE: A very smooth touchdown.

HOUSTON: Eagle, you are stay for T1. [The first step in the lunar operation.] Over.

TRANQUILITY BASE: Roger. Stay for T1.

HOUSTON: Roger and we see you venting the ox[idizer].

TRANQUILITY BASE: Roger.

COLUMBIA (the command and service module): How do you read me?

HOUSTON: Columbia, he has landed Tranquility Base. Eagle is at Tranquility. I read you five by. Over.

COLUMBIA: Yes, I heard the whole thing.

HOUSTON: Well, it's a good show.

COLUMBIA: Fantastic.

TRANQUILITY BASE: I'll second that.

Aldrin Describes the Moonscape

TRANQUILITY BASE: We'll get to the details of what's around here but it looks like a collection of just about every variety of shape, angularity, granularity, about every variety of rock you could find. The colors vary pretty much depending on how you are looking relative to the zero phase length. There doesn't appear to be too much of a general color at all. However, it looks as though some of the rocks and boulders, of which there are quite a few in the near area—it looks as though they're going to have some interesting colors to them. Over.

HOUSTON: Roger. Copy. Sounds good to us, Tranquility. We'll let you press on through the simulated countdown and we'll talk to you later. Over.

TRANQUILITY BASE: Okay, this one-sixth G is just like an airplane.

HOUSTON: Roger, Tranquility. Be advised there are lots of smiling faces in this room and all over the world. Over.

TRANQUILITY BASE: There are two of them up here.

HOUSTON: Roger. It was a beautiful job, you guys.

COLUMBIA: And don't forget one in the command module.

TRANQUILITY BASE: Roger.

Columbia in Communication with Tranquility Base

APOLLO CONTROL: That last remark from Mike Collins at an altitude of 60 miles. The comments on the landing, on the manual take-over came from Neil Armstrong. Buzz Aldrin followed that with a description of the lunar surface and the rocks and boulders that they are able to see out the window of the LM [lunar module].

COLUMBIA: Thanks for putting me on relay, Houston. I was missing all the action.

HOUSTON: Roger. We'll enable relay.

COLUMBIA (4:30 P.M.): I just got it, I think.

HOUSTON: Roger, Columbia. This is Houston. Say something; they ought to be able to hear you. Over.

COLUMBIA: Roger. Tranquility Base. It sure sounded great from up here. You guys did a fantastic job.

TRANQUILITY BASE: Thank you. Just keep that orbiting base ready for us up there, now.

COLUMBIA: Will do. . . .

Adapting to Gravity, Describing Surface Appearance

APOLLO CONTROL: Neil Armstrong reporting there is no difficulty adapting to the one-sixth gravity of the moon.

TRANQUILITY BASE: [Unintelligible] . . . window, with relatively level plain cratered with fairly a large number of craters of the 5- to 50-foot variety. And some ridges, small, 20 to 30 feet high, I would guess. And literally thousands of little one- and two-foot craters around the area. We see some angular blocks out several hundred feet in front of us that are probably two feet in size and have angular edges. There is a hill in view just about on the ground track ahead of us. Difficult to estimate, but might be a half a mile or a mile.

HOUSTON: Roger, Tranquility. We copy. Over.

COLUMBIA: Sounds like it looks a lot better than it did yesterday. At that very low sun angle, it looked rough as a cob then.

TRANQUILITY BASE: It really was rough, Mike, over the targeted landing area. It was extremely rough, cratered and large numbers of rocks that were probably some many larger than 5 or 10 feet in size.

COLUMBIA: When in doubt, land long.

TRANQUILITY BASE: Well, we did.

COLUMBIA: Do you have any idea whether they landed left or right of center line—just a little bit long. Is that all we know?

HOUSTON: Apparently that's about all we can tell. Over.

COLUMBIA: Okay, thank you.

TRANQUILITY BASE: Okay. I'd say the color of the local surface is very comparable to that we observed from orbit at this sun angle—about 10 degrees sun angle or that nature. It's pretty much without color. It's gray and it's very white as you look into the zero phase line. And it's considerably darker gray, more like an ashen gray, as you look out 90 degrees to the sun. Some of the surface rocks in close here that have been fractured or disturbed by the rocket engine plume are coated with this light gray on the outside. But where they've been broken, they display a dark, very dark, gray interior and it looks like it could be country basalt. . . .

Armstrong Steps Out onto the Moon Surface

ARMSTRONG: Okay, Houston, I'm on the porch.

HOUSTON: Roger, Neil.

HOUSTON: Columbia, Columbia, This is Houston. One minute, 30 seconds LOS, all systems go, Over.

ALDRIN: Halt where you a minute. Neil.

ARMSTRONG AND ALDRIN: Okay. Everything's nice and straight in here. Okay, can you pull the door open a little more? Right.

HOUSTON: We're getting a picture on the TV.

Edwin E. Aldrin Jr., pictured above, and Neil Armstrong, made history as the first men to walk on the moon.

ALDRIN: You've got a good picture, huh?

HOUSTON: There's a great deal of contrast in it and currently it's upside down on monitor. But we can make out a fair amount of detail.

ARMSTRONG: Okay, will you verify the position, the opening I ought to have on the camera.

HOUSTON: The what? We can see you coming down the ladder now.

ARMSTRONG: Okay. I just checked getting back up to that first step. It didn't collapse too far. But it's adequate to get back up. It's a pretty good little jump.

ARMSTRONG: I'm at the foot of the ladder. The LM foot beds are only depressed in the surface about one or two inches, although the surface appears to be very, very fine-grained as you get close to it. It's almost like a powder. It's very fine. I'm going to step off the LM now. That's one small step for man, one giant leap for mankind.

The surface is fine and powdery. I can pick it up loosely with my toe. It does adhere in fine layers like powdered charcoal to the sole and the sides of my boots. I only go in a small fraction of an inch, maybe an eighth of an inch but I can see the footprints of my boots and the treads in the fine sandy particles.

There seems to be no difficulty in moving around this and we suspect that it's even perhaps easier than the simulations of 1/6 G that we performed in various simulations on the ground. Actually no trouble to walk around.

The descent engine did not leave a crater of any size. It has about one foot clearance on the ground. We're essentially on a very level place here. I can see some evidence of rays emanating from the descent engine, but a very insignificant amount. Okay, Buzz, are we ready to bring down the camera?

ALDRIN: I'm all ready. I think it's squared away and in good shape. But you'll have to pay out all the LEC. Looks like it's coming out nice and evenly. It's quite dark here in the shadow and a little hard for me to see if I have good footing. I'll work my way over into the sunlight here without looking directly into the sun.

ARMSTRONG: Looking up at the LM, I'm standing directly in the shadow now looking up at . . . in the windows and I can see everything quite clearly. The light is sufficiently bright back-lighted into the front of the LM that everything is clearly visible. I'll step out and take some of my first pictures here.

ALDRIN: Are you going to get the contingency sample? Okay. That's good.

ARMSTRONG: The contingency sample is down and it's up. Like it's a little difficult to dig through the crust. It's very interesting. It's a very soft surface but here and there where I plug with the contingency sample collector I run into very hard surface but it appears to be very cohesive material of the same sort. I'll try to get a rock in here.

HOUSTON: Oh, that looks beautiful from here, Neil.

ARMSTRONG: It has a stark beauty all its own. It's like much of the high desert of the United States. It's different but it's very pretty out here. Be advised that a lot of the rock samples out here, the hard rock samples have what appears to be vesicles in the surface.

ARMSTRONG: This has been about six or eight inches into the surface. It's easy to push on it. I'm sure I could push it in farther but it's hard for me to bend down farther than that.

ALDRIN: Ready for me to come out?

ARMSTRONG: Yeah. Just stand by a second, I'll move this over the handrail.

ALDRIN: Okay?

ARMSTRONG: All right, that's got it. Are you ready?

ALDRIN: All set.

ARMSTRONG: Okay. You saw what difficulties I was having. I'll try to watch your PLSS [portable life support system] from underneath here. The toes are about to come over the sill. Now drop your PLSS down. There you go, you're clear. And laterally you're good. About an inch clearance on top of your PLSS. You need a little bit of arching of the back to come down.

ALDRIN: How far are my feet from the . . .

ARMSTRONG: You're right at the edge of the porch.

ALDRIN: Small little foot movement. Porch. Arching of the back . . . without any trouble at all.

ALDRIN: Now I want to back up and partially close the hatch—making sure not to lock it on my way out.

ARMSTRONG: Good thought. . . .

ALDRIN: That's our home for the next couple of hours; we want to take care of it. I'm on the top step. It's a very simple matter to hop down from one step to the next.

ARMSTRONG: Yes, I found that to be very comfortable, and walking is also very comfortable, Houston. You've got three more steps and then a long one.

ALDRIN: I'm going to leave that one foot up there and both hands down to about the fourth rung up.

ARMSTRONG: A little more. About another inch, there you got it. That's a good step.

ALDRIN: About a three footer. Beautiful view.

ARMSTRONG: Ain't that somethin'?

Roe v. Wade Legalizes Abortion in All Fifty
States: January 22, 1973

The Controversy and the Impact of *Roe v. Wade*

by Lawrence M. Friedman

As soon as the Supreme Court announced its decision that abortion was legal in the United States, a firestorm of controversy exploded. Groups immediately organized in support of, or to protest, abortion. The Catholic Church was, and still is, a major proponent of the "pro-life" movement. Feminist organizations were, and still are, major supporters of the "pro-choice" movement. For thirty years, both sides have remained passionate about their beliefs and have kept up the legal fight to advance their positions. Although abortion is still legal, the pro-life advocates have succeeded in getting stricter laws passed regarding parental consent and medical reporting.

In more practical terms, every state had to reevaluate and change its laws regulating abortion after *Roe v. Wade.* Fifteen states had to adjust their laws substantially, and thirty-one states had to start over with brand-new laws. Some figures cite about two hundred bills passing through state legislatures in 1973. At the federal level, efforts were made to introduce constitutional amendments to address the issue specifically. Clinics providing abortions also felt the change in a big way. Demand grew quickly; in 1972 approximately five hundred thousand abortions were performed annually, but by the late 1980s that number had tripled.

In the following excerpt Lawrence M. Friedman, a professor at Stanford Law School, reviews the legal and social issues surrounding *Roe v. Wade*. Friedman is an award-winning researcher and professor who specializes in the history of American law and its consequences.

T he *Roe v. Wade* decision was controversial in 1973, and it is just as controversial today—if not more so. Few cases have led to as much hot and bitter debate. For parallels, one may have to reach back to *Brown v. Board of Education* [a case that led to desegregation of public schools], or perhaps all the way to *Dred Scott* [a case where it was ruled that slaves born to slaves could not be citizens]. *Roe v. Wade* belongs to a very select club of Supreme Court decisions—those that sent shock waves through the country, affecting every aspect of political life. How one assesses this impact, and its political consequences, depends in part on how one looks at *Roe v. Wade*. Does it lie outside the mainstream of constitutional doctrine? Or is it not out of line—for the present epoch at least—in doctrine or theory?

What was it about *Roe v. Wade* that touched off such a storm of comment and criticism? Some critics claim to be bothered not by the outcome, but by what they consider poor craftsmanship. For others the objection is more fundamental. They challenge the very legitimacy of *Roe*. They find no warrant in the Constitution for what the Court did; abortion, they think, has no business parading before society as a constitutional issue. Louis Lusky has described *Roe v. Wade*, sneeringly, as "freehand constitutionmaking." Other scholars have said even worse things about it. Senator Jesse Helms summarized the views of seven eminent constitutional scholars, who all expressed "shock and dismay" over the reasoning of the Court. Helms was able to fill his statement with quotes that condemned the case: it was a mere "political judgment," or even "the most outrageous decision ever handed down by the Court."

Of course, many scholars defend the decision. Some of these take a position which is almost the polar opposite. They are dismayed by attempts to undo *Roe v. Wade* by amending the Constitution. They, too, talk about legitimacy, but for them it is such an amendment that would be illegitimate. Abortion, they say, does not belong in our written Constitution, which should stick to more fundamental matters. . . .

Social Relevance of the Court's Decision-Making

The Supreme Court picks its cases; but it picks them from among the hundreds that come up from below, clamoring for attention. These cases, in the aggregate, represent what troubles society. In a sense, then, the court's agenda is always fresh. It is always a kind of menu of issues, faithful more or less to what is brewing in society.

Griswold [a case that legalized birth control] and *Roe* are about social issues; indeed, the abortion decision is perhaps the key social issue today. But exactly what is the issue? A good way to begin is to define what it is not. It is not permissiveness as such, or the vexed question of sexual morality. At any rate, that is not what the Supreme Court is up to. There is no evidence that the Court wants to read the "sexual revolution" into the Constitution, or to discover the philosophy of *Playboy* magazine hidden in the text of the Fourteenth Amendment. The Court is not even embracing the old-fashioned liberalism of John Stuart Mill. Nor is it accepting, as dogma or working principle, the idea that whatever consenting adults do to or with each other in private and without violence is beyond the reach of the state.

Indeed, Thomas Grey, in his insightful essay, argues that the Court is playing a rather conservative game. It is trying to preserve family values in a confused and complicated world. The contraception and abortion cases, he says, are "dedicated to the cause of social stability through the reinforcement of traditional institutions." They have "nothing to do with the sexual liberation of the individual. The contraception and abortion cases are simply family planning cases." In particular, they represent a "standard conservative" view, that "family stability is threatened by unwanted pregnancies."

On issues of sex, marriage, abortion, and the rest, there are, of course, all sorts of views in society; and we can label these views (with some rough accuracy) as right, left, and various degrees of middle. The Supreme Court—judging from the results of its decisions—lies somewhere in the middle of the range of opinion. It is of course light-years away from the fundamentalists in the Bible Belt, yet Grey's point is still a good one. The Supreme

Court has shown sympathy and respect for traditional family values. It recognizes, however, that today's traditional family is different from yesterday's and has to be different to survive.

What the justices think about social issues may be less important than what they think about the role of their court. Here we have to read the record carefully and between the lines. (Often one does best by refusing to read the opinions at all, on the grounds that outcomes tell more about what the justices are up to than do endless pages of constitutional "filler.") The justices seem to feel that cases like *Griswold* and *Wade* have a special quality that sets them apart from other public issues. In some significant way, society should not or cannot trust the usual decisionmakers (legislators, for example) in these affairs. . . .

Resistance to Change in the Legal System

In a pluralist system there are many laws that could not now be passed as an initial matter and yet cannot now be repealed. On some highly controverted subjects, the status quo is frozen; to move up or down, forward or backward, is politically dangerous. Major abortion law falls in that class. The only safe course is doing nothing. In 1973, it was hard to move on abortion in any direction. For the most part this is still true a decade later. Despite the activity of pro-life groups and the support of the president, antiabortion law moves very slowly in Congress. There is more action in the states, but hardly a landslide. New laws show recalcitrance, but not outright defiance. The most sensitive issues are those that touch on the rights of parents. Teenage sex clearly troubles people far more than whether a husband and wife decide on an abortion. Legislators, on the whole (one suspects), would be pleased if the whole issue could somehow go away.

There is a package of social issues about which people are likely to hide their real feelings. Pornography is one. Prostitution is another. Both are big businesses. Few people speak up for them, certainly few congressmen. That there are so many customers, however, means there is a large, hidden interest group, whose impact is felt but not heard. Abortion may not be in the same camp, but there are definite similarities. Few people are *for* abortion. Rather, they accept it as a necessary evil. The arguments against abortion are direct, simple, and to the point. The arguments for it are indirect and complicated. There are less arguments for abortion than against forbidding it, and for reasons other than the merits of abortion. (Similarly, very few people defend pornography. Instead, they defend the right of free speech, and try to sneak pornography into this tent.)

The court's opinion in *Roe v. Wade* seems to take these factors into account. It was an attempt to wipe out what the Court considered outmoded taboos, in a field where, for various political and social reasons, legislative action was difficult, if not impossible; to frame a relatively clearcut, objective rule; to compromise between extremists on both sides; and to put the issue to rest. These were old and useful aims, by and large, that had worked many times before. *Griswold*, for example, is a case in point. By 1973, contraception was hardly an issue. The Court had helped put it to rest.

The Response to *Roe v. Wade*

What *Roe* did, in essence, was to take a social problem and reduce it to a legal problem, at least in form. The technique does not always work. It failed in *Dred Scott*, for example. But there the Court failed because it came out on the wrong side of the issue, not because of form or technique. The solution was unacceptable to a large, passionate, committed group of people. The Court can do a lot, but it cannot control passions that run deep enough to bring on war. The abortion decision may be of this type, but there is good reason to doubt it.

I have argued that the abortion case did not come out of the blue. It rested on a base of prior law. The prior law was rather porous and spongy, but it was there, at least from *Griswold* on. The Court did not jump into the abortion decision feet first. It went slowly and carefully, did considerable soul-searching, and came out with a decision that in form was highly legalistic. The Court acted, as it always does, in the classic common-law way, building on the base of the past.

The abortion issue, however, turned out to be more difficult than the Court expected. The decision provoked enormous controversy. The reaction was volcanic—a slow rumble, followed by eruptions. No one predicted so strong a response. Yet after a decade, the controversy is still essentially legal and electoral. Nobody has taken to the street. Compared to the aftermath of *Brown v. Board of Education*, for example, the reaction to *Roe v. Wade*—for all its sound and fury—has been relatively toothless. There has been no special, thorough attack on the Court—not, at any rate, because of this case alone. There are some proposals to tinker with its jurisdiction. But the Court has not been a lightning rod for accumulated furies, as was true of the race cases. The reaction, in short, although loud and continuous, has also been solidly normal and well within the ground rules of debate. There is no reason to doubt it will continue to be so.

Roe v. Wade Shaped Subsequent Decisions

The abortion cases after *Roe* show the Court in a cautious mood. This may have helped to defuse the controversy. The Court stuck to its guns at first. In *Planned Parenthood of Missouri v. Danforth*, the Court confronted a Missouri law passed a year after *Roe*. Among other things, it required a married woman to get her husband's consent before an abortion. Unmarried women under eighteen had to get parental consent. The Court struck down these rules. Another part of the statute outlawed "saline amniocentesis, as a method or technique of abortion, after the first twelve weeks of pregnancy." This was, in fact, the most common technique in medical use at the time. The Court struck down this restriction too. It was "unreasonable"—a "regulation designed to inhibit . . . the vast majority of abortions after the first twelve weeks." Six justices joined in the decision one way or another. The *Wade* court held firm, except for the chief justice.

Firmness (of a sort) also characterized *Bellotti v. Baird*, a case which involved the vexing question of abortion for teenaged girls. A Massachusetts law, enacted against the background of *Danforth*, required the consent of the girls' parents. If "one or both" refused, a judge of the superior court could give consent, "for good cause shown, after such hearing as he deems necessary." The Massachusetts legislature was obviously trying to discourage abortion and to make a statement about parents' rights, the family, and the like. The Court did not go along. The statute was, in effect, labeled a nice try, but it fell "short of constitutional standards in certain respects." Every minor must have the right "to go directly to a court without first consulting or notifying her parents." If she convinces the court that she is "mature" and can make an "intelligent" abortion choice on her own, the court "must" allow her to act, "without parental consultation or consent."

The case had no real majority opinion. The language quoted came from Justice Lewis F. Powell, Jr., joined by the chief justice [Warren Burger], Potter Stewart, and (surprisingly) William H. Rehnquist, who had been a dissenter in both *Roe* and *Danforth*, but was willing to go along with the Court as long as *Danforth* lasted. Another group of four justices concurred in the result. Only Justice Byron R. White dissented. The various opinions refer at times to the "constitutional right" to have an abortion, but the Constitution itself is not cited. This is yet another sign of what one might call the common-law approach to constitutional law. The abortion case grew out of the *Griswold* line and then established a new starting point, on which still later cases built, one on top of the other. This method is time-honored, a classic technique of legal evolution. Constitutional theory tends to ignore it, and constitutional decisions are supposed to be special, because they rest on a text, and a sacred one at that. But the actual process of decision is much the same as in other fields of law.

The latest word [as of 1983], and a most ambiguous one, came in 1981 in *H.L. v. Matheson*, a case from Utah. This too had to do with the duty to notify parents. The plaintiff wanted the Court to strike down the Utah statute but the Court dodged the issue. The opinion, written by Chief Justice Warren E. Burger, upheld the statute as it applied to the plaintiff, a girl who lived with her parents, was not emancipated, and made "no claim or showing as to her maturity or . . . her relations with her parents." For such people, the statute was constitutional, and the Court did not have to ask whether the law was offensive when applied to young women in other situations. The case looks like a cautious, strategic retreat from the exposed ground occupied in *Bellotti*, but nobody can be sure as yet where the Court is going.

The cases clearly are part of a complex ritual dance between the Court and the state legislatures. Massachusetts, Missouri, Utah, and other states had been squirming and wriggling to find ways around some aspects of *Roe v. Wade*. The states used standard methods—methods that are, in the long run, fairly innocuous. Essentially, the legislatures comb through opinions, looking for chinks in the armor. The results, even when the Court accepts them, are a kind of compromise: for example, teenage versus adult abortion. . . .

How Permanent Is *Roe v. Wade?*

What is the future of abortion law? There are proposals to strip federal courts of jurisdiction in abortion cases, but these seem doomed to fail. *Roe v. Wade* will continue to be the law unless the Supreme Court overrules itself or is overruled by constitutional amendment or otherwise. One mechanism to turn the Court around is a proposed statute that would declare, as the sense of Congress, that human life exists from the moment of conception. Congress is empowered to enforce the Fourteenth Amendment by appropriate legislation; thus Congress could (arguably) prohibit abortion as a way of protecting "life." If the Court went along, this would be the end of *Roe v. Wade.*

This seems too tricky a route to those who favor formal constitutional amendment, a more cumbersome but forthright technique. An amendment to the Constitution would at least eliminate one imponderable, namely, whether the Court would uphold a human life bill as constitutional. Supporters of the statutory approach think constitutional amendment is too slow and too likely to fail. And some opponents of abortion, like former Secretary of Health, Education, and Welfare Joseph A. Califano, feel that constitutional amendment would be somehow inappropriate. "We have to stop running to the Constitution to solve all of our problems," Califano has said.

Is it out of bounds to write abortion into the Constitution? This question cannot be sensibly answered as a matter of theory. What is appropriate for a constitution is whatever is perceived as fundamental and important. The Constitution protects life, liberty, and property. For those who feel strongly that abortion is murder, it is absurd to argue that the subject is not appropriate. Understandably, the pro-choice people oppose an abortion amendment and use all arguments, including those of constitutional purity. As I noted earlier, it was the Court that put the abortion issue into the Constitution. The opponents have no choice but to fight on the battlefield imposed on them. The real issue, the issue that cannot be avoided, is the morality and social utility of abortion itself.

Justice Harry Blackmun Explains the Court's Controversial Decision

by Harry Blackmun

Prior to the landmark Supreme Court decision *Roe v. Wade*, popular opinion about abortion was already shifting. In the past, abortions had been unsafe, and statutes existed to protect women. As a result, these statutes prosecuted doctors, not women. However, with modern medical advances and social changes for women, such as the availability of the birth control pill, new career opportunities, and increased political visibility (women were active in protests during the 1960s and 1970s), a growing segment of society was ready for increased availability of abortions.

When twenty-one-year-old Norma McCorvey found herself divorced, out of work, and pregnant, she sought an abortion. McCorvey's parents were already rearing her five-year-old daughter, and she did not feel that she could become a mother again. Unable to find a doctor willing to provide the abortion in Texas, where it was illegal except to save the mother's life, McCorvey met Linda Coffee and Sarah Weddington. Coffee and Weddington were two attorneys

---

Harry Blackmun, "Opinion of the Court," *Roe v. Wade*, 410 U.S. 113 (1973).

anxious for a test case to challenge the Texas statute.

Coffee and Weddington challenged the statute on the grounds of right to privacy. Previous cases had established that any rights not specifically mentioned in the Constitution are rights held by the people and that privacy rights apply to marriage relationships and having children.

The case advanced all the way to the Supreme Court, where Mc-Corvey (the appellant, using the pseudonym "Jane Roe") had her case heard by the seven sitting justices. The defendant was Henry Wade (the appellee), Texas's Dallas County district attorney. After hearing both arguments in December 1971, the justices agreed that the case needed a full Court of nine, and so after two justices were appointed to the empty seats, the case was heard again in October 1972. Justice Harry Blackmun delivered the majority opinion of the Court on January 22, 1973.

In a seven-to-two ruling in McCorvey's favor, the Court declared that abortion would be legalized in the United States. They believed that the right to privacy applied but was not absolute. The Court stated that in the first trimester, women were empowered to make decisions about abortions; in the second trimester, the state could enforce certain restrictions for the mother's health; and in the third trimester, states could refuse abortions except to save the life of the mother. The following excerpts from the actual Court opinion describe the justices' reasoning.

MR. JUSTICE BLACKMUN delivered the opinion of the Court. . . .

The Texas statutes that concern us here are Arts. 1191–1194 and 1196 of the State's Penal Code. These make it a crime to "procure an abortion," as therein defined, or to attempt one, except with respect to "an abortion procured or attempted by medical advice for the purpose of saving the life of the mother." Similar statutes are in existence in a majority of the States.

Texas first enacted a criminal abortion statute in 1854. Texas Laws 1854, c. 49, [Section] 1, set forth in 3 H. Gammel, Laws of Texas 1502 (1898). This was soon modified into language that has remained substantially unchanged to the present time. See Texas Penal Code of 1857, c. 7, Arts. 531–536; G. Paschal, Laws of Texas, Arts. 2192–2197 (1866); Texas Rev.Stat., c. 8, Arts. 536–541 (1879); Texas Rev.Crim.Stat., Arts. 1071–1076 (1911). The final article in each of these compilations provided the same exception, as does the present Article 1196, for an abortion by "medical advice for the purpose of saving the life of the mother."

Review of Roe's Case

Jane Roe, a single woman who was residing in Dallas County, Texas, instituted this federal action in March 1970 against the District Attorney of the county. She sought a declaratory judgment that the Texas criminal abortion statutes were unconstitutional on their face, and an injunction restraining the defendant from enforcing the statutes.

Roe alleged that she was unmarried and pregnant; that she wished to terminate her pregnancy by an abortion "performed by a competent, licensed physician, under safe, clinical conditions"; that she was unable to get a "legal" abortion in Texas because her life did not appear to be threatened by the continuation of her pregnancy; and that she could not afford to travel to another jurisdiction in order to secure a legal abortion under safe conditions. She claimed that the Texas statutes were unconstitutionally vague and that they abridged her right of personal privacy, protected by the First, Fourth, Fifth, Ninth, and Fourteenth Amendments. By an amendment to her complaint, Roe purported to sue "on behalf of herself and all other women" similarly situated. . . .

Right to Privacy Includes Abortion

The Constitution does not explicitly mention any right of privacy. In a line of decisions, however, going back perhaps as far as *Union Pacific R. Co. v. Botsford* (1891), the Court has recognized that a right of personal privacy, or a guarantee of certain areas or zones of privacy, does exist under the Constitution. In varying contexts, the Court or individual Justices have, indeed, found at least the roots of that right in the First Amendment. . . . These decisions make it clear that only personal rights that can be deemed "fundamental" or "implicit in the concept of ordered liberty," *Palko v. Connecticut* (1937), are included in this guarantee of personal privacy. They also make it clear that the right has some extension to activities relating to marriage, . . . procreation, . . . contraception, . . . family relationships, . . . and childrearing and education. . . .

This right of privacy, whether it be founded in the Fourteenth Amendment's concept of personal liberty and restrictions upon state action, as we feel it is, or, as the District Court determined, in the Ninth Amendment's reservation of rights to the people, is broad enough to encompass a woman's decision whether or not to terminate her pregnancy. The detriment that the State would impose upon the pregnant woman by denying this choice altogether is apparent. Specific and direct harm medically diagnosable even in early pregnancy may be involved. Maternity, or additional offspring, may force upon the woman a distressful life and future. Psychological harm may be imminent. Mental and physical health may be taxed by child care. There is also the distress, for all concerned, associated with the unwanted child, and there is the problem of bringing a child into a family already unable, psychologically and otherwise, to care for it. In other cases, as in this one, the additional difficulties and continuing stigma of unwed motherhood may be involved. All these are factors the woman and her responsible physician necessarily will consider in consultation.

The Right to Privacy, However, Is Not Absolute

On the basis of elements such as these, appellant and some amici argue that the woman's right is absolute and that she is entitled to terminate her pregnancy at whatever time, in whatever way, and for whatever reason she alone chooses. With this we do not agree. Appellant's arguments that Texas either has no valid interest at all in regulating the abortion decision, or no interest strong enough to support any limitation upon the woman's sole determination, are unpersuasive. The Court's decisions recognizing a right of privacy also acknowledge that some state regulation in areas protected by that right is appropriate. As noted above, a State may properly assert important interests in safeguarding health, in maintaining medical standards, and in protecting potential life. At some point in pregnancy, these respective interests become sufficiently compelling to sustain regulation of the factors that govern the abortion decision. The privacy right involved, therefore, cannot be said to be absolute. In fact, it is not clear to us that the claim asserted by some amici that one has an unlimited right to do with one's body as one pleases bears a close relationship to the right of privacy previously articulated in the

Court's decisions. The Court has refused to recognize an unlimited right of this kind in the past. *Jacobson v. Massachusetts* (1905) (vaccination); *Buck v. Bell* (1927) (sterilization).

We, therefore, conclude that the right of personal privacy includes the abortion decision, but that this right is not unqualified, and must be considered against important state interests in regulation. . . .

Defining "Person" in the Constitution

The District Court held that the appellee failed to meet his burden of demonstrating that the Texas statute's infringement upon Roe's rights was necessary to support a compelling state interest, and that, although the appellee presented "several compelling justifications for state presence in the area of abortions," the statutes outstripped these justifications and swept "far beyond any areas of compelling state interest." 314 F. Supp. at 1222–1223. Appellant and appellee both contest that holding. Appellant, as has been indicated, claims an absolute right that bars any state imposition of criminal penalties in the area. Appellee argues that the State's determination to recognize and protect prenatal life from and after conception constitutes a compelling state interest. As noted above, we do not agree fully with either formulation.

A. The appellee and certain amici argue that the fetus is a "person" within the language and meaning of the Fourteenth Amendment. In support of this, they outline at length and in detail the well known facts of fetal development. If this suggestion of personhood is established, the appellant's case, of course, collapses, for the fetus' right to life would then be guaranteed specifically by the Amendment. The appellant conceded as much on reargument. On the other hand, the appellee conceded on reargument that no case could be cited that holds that a fetus is a person within the meaning of the Fourteenth Amendment.

The Constitution does not define "person" in so many words. Section 1 of the Fourteenth Amendment contains three references to "person." The first, in defining "citizens," speaks of "persons born or naturalized in the United States." The word also appears both in the Due Process Clause and in the Equal Protection Clause. . . . But in nearly all these instances, the use of the word is such that it has application only post-natally. None indicates, with any assurance, that it has any possible pre-natal application.

All this, together with our observation, *supra*, that, throughout the major portion of the 19th century, prevailing legal abortion practices were far freer than they are today, persuades us that the word "person," as used in the Fourteenth Amendment, does not include the unborn. . . .

The State's Responsibility to the Mother

We do not agree that, by adopting one theory of life, Texas may override the rights of the pregnant woman that are at stake. We repeat, however, that the State does have an important and legitimate interest in preserving and protecting the health of the pregnant woman, whether she be a resident of the State or a nonresident who seeks medical consultation and treatment there, and that it has still another important and legitimate interest in protecting the potentiality of human life. These interests are separate and distinct. Each grows in substantiality as the woman approaches term and, at a point during pregnancy, each becomes "compelling."

With respect to the State's important and legitimate interest in the health of the mother, the "compelling" point, in the light of present medical knowledge, is at approximately the end of the first trimester. This is so because of the now-established medical fact, that, until the end of the first trimester mortality in abortion may be less than mortality in normal childbirth. It follows that, from and after this point, a State may regulate the abortion procedure to the extent that the regulation reasonably relates to the preservation and protection of maternal health. Examples of permissible state regulation in this area are requirements as to the qualifications of the person who is to perform the abortion; as to the licensure of that person; as to the facility in which the procedure is to be performed, that is, whether it must be a hospital or may be a clinic or some other place of less-than-hospital status; as to the licensing of the facility; and the like.

New Parameters of Legal Abortions

This means, on the other hand, that, for the period of pregnancy prior to this "compelling" point, the attending physician, in consultation with his patient, is free to determine, without regulation by the State, that, in his medical judgment, the patient's pregnancy should be terminated. If that decision is reached, the judgment may be effectuated by an abortion free of interference by the State.

With respect to the State's important and legitimate interest in potential life, the "compelling" point is at viability. This is so because the fetus then presumably has the capability of meaningful life outside the mother's womb. State regulation protective of fetal life after viability thus has both logical and biological justifications. If the State is interested in protecting fetal life after viability, it may go so far as to proscribe abortion during that period, except when it is necessary to preserve the life or health of the mother.

Measured against these standards, Art. 1196 of the Texas Penal Code, in restricting legal abortions to those "procured or attempted by medical advice for the purpose of saving the life of the mother," sweeps too broadly. The statute makes no distinction between abortions performed early in pregnancy and those performed later, and it limits to a single reason, "saving" the mother's life, the legal justification for the procedure. The statute, therefore, cannot survive the constitutional attack made upon it here.

10

**President Richard Nixon Resigns:
August 8, 1974**

Nixon Resigns

by Stanley I. Kutler

In the history of the United States, only two presidents have ever been impeached: Andrew Johnson in the 1860s and Bill Clinton in the 1990s. When Congress passes articles of impeachment, a president is, in effect, placed on trial. If two-thirds of the Senate finds the president guilty, he can be removed from office.

Richard Nixon faced the threat of impeachment in the summer of 1974. By that time the Watergate investigators had heard the Oval Office tape of June 23, 1972, which indicated that Nixon had been involved in the Watergate cover-up.

In the following selection from his book *The Wars of Watergate: The Last Crisis of Richard Nixon*, Stanley I. Kutler explores Nixon's decision to resign as president of the United States effective August 9, 1974. Even though he had stated in his January 1974 State of the Union Address that he would never resign, and even though he had many supporters, Nixon knew that he would lose any formal impeachment hearings in the Senate. In order to avoid further damage to the nation and to the Republican Party, writes Kutler, Nixon decided to step down. Kutler is the E. Gordon Fox Professor of American Institutions at the University of Wisconsin.

President Nixon appeared for his last Cabinet meeting on Tuesday, August 6. As usual, the staff prepared "talking points" for him. Whatever decisions had been reached—tentatively or firmly—the President dealt with the group as he always had: as subordinates whom he needed to exhort to do their best in behalf of the Administration. He had, nevertheless, to confront the impeachment issue and give the Cabinet officers

Stanley I. Kutler, *The Wars of Watergate: The Last Crisis of Richard Nixon*. New York: Alfred A. Knopf, 1990. Copyright © 1990 by Stanley I. Kutler. Reproduced by permission of the publisher.

some indication of his course. He reminded his lieutenants that the presidency had experienced enormous trauma in the past decade, with the assassination of Kennedy and with Johnson "literally hounded from office." The institution, he said, must not sustain another "hammer blow" without a defense. Consequently, he would not resign, and would let the constitutional process run. This, he insisted, would be in the "best interests of the Nation"; he would not "desert the principles which give our government legitimacy." To do otherwise, he continued, "would be a regrettable departure from American historical principles." He offered nothing in the way of personal defense aside from past diplomatic triumphs; instead, he wrapped himself in the mantle of the presidency—claiming that he had no choice but to continue the route designed in the Constitution.

With that, Nixon turned to a discussion of economic problems, projecting policies for six months in the future. Attorney General William Saxbe was dumbfounded by Nixon's bravado. "Mr. President, don't you think we should be talking about next week, not next year?" he asked. According to Saxbe, Nixon looked around the table, no one said a word, and with that he picked up his papers and left the room.

Nixon Wanted Impeachment at First

The President's line was familiar. He had said in his January 1974 State of the Union message that he never would resign. He had told himself on numerous occasions that resignation could only be equated with guilt. In an interview with columnist James Kilpatrick in May, Nixon vehemently denied any intention of resigning. To do so, he said, would be to fatally weaken the presidency. Future presidents, he warned, would constantly be looking over their shoulders at Congress. Resignation or impeachment, he continued, would destabilize the nation and the world. Either path "would have the traumatic effect of destroying that sense of stability and leadership. And as far as this particular President is concerned, I will not be a party under any circumstances to any action which would set that kind of precedent."

Nixon thought then that he must let the impeachment process run its course because it would be "best for the country, our system of government, and the constitutional process." Two months later, Representative Caldwell Butler came to the same conclusion. Resignation offered only short-term benefits, Butler thought; more important, he did not want to establish a precedent "for harassment out of office, which is what would be claimed." He, too, wanted to follow the constitutional process: "It's a pretty good system." The President at that time gave every appearance of continuing in office. He asked an old friend to "leisurely" prepare a speech on world law and peace. Nixon wanted it as a radio address but then proposed a wide mail distribution. He planned the talk for August or September, and he emphasized there was no need for urgency.

Old friends weighed in with encouraging words. A New York lawyer exhorted Nixon not to resign and bitterly assailed "gutless Republicans" who had suggested such a course. She urged him to have the "courage and fortitude" to go through the constitutional process. Some religious supporters urged the same course but with a different twist which apparently received no consideration. The Reverend Norman Vincent Peale relayed and endorsed a message from the prominent Jewish Orthodox leader Rabbi Samuel Silver, of Cincinnati. The nation, Silver believed, wanted to "love" its President. "All he needs to say is that he is sorry for the whole thing, that he admits he didn't handle it too well, that he is only human and he regrets the bad habit of swearing, etc.; that he should have cracked down on any wrongdoing immediately, that he hates to hurt people; that all he asks is the forgiveness of the people." Silver added that the President need not act like a "worm." But he must offer "a good, honest, humble attitude of contrition."

Even after the revelations of the June 23, 1972, tape, the President received extraordinary gestures of support. A California restaurateur, who had sent the President $10,000 to help him pay his income taxes, offered to turn over his interest in twenty-nine restaurants to finance a defense. "I love Richard Nixon—he is the greatest President this country has ever had," he declared. An Indiana Republican Congressman offered the same sentiments on the *Today* television show on August 8. "Don't confuse me with the facts. I've got a closed mind," Representative Earl Landgrebe said in response to the question whether he would vote to impeach the President. He would "stick with" Nixon, even if "I have to be taken out of this building and shot. . . . President Nixon has been the greatest President this country has had." But after the "smoking gun" tape became public, James Kilpatrick could take no more. "I am close to tears," he wrote. "Nixon's duplicity is almost beyond bearing." Had he told the truth from the outset, Kilpatrick declared, Watergate would have been a nine-day wonder, Nixon would have been re-elected, and no more would have been heard of the affair. Kilpatrick had believed the President when he said he knew nothing of the cover-up and that he was not a crook. Now, he sadly concluded, "it no longer really matters. . . . My President is a liar. I wish he were a crook instead."

Nixon's Party and Staff Begin to Abandon Him

But Richard Nixon was nothing if not a seasoned political hand. He had heard rumors for months that congressional Republicans might view his resignation as a relief from the terrible onus of voting on impeachment and as the way to remove the President as a political albatross for the party. Nixon undoubtedly had put his personal concerns above those of his party; yet, for all his disdain, he knew that he still had to reckon with it as a force of political life. He knew that winning was everything, and he offered a political twist to the sports metaphors he often favored when he noted that generosity or magnanimity had little to do with the outcome of events: "The burden of the wounded must be removed in order for the rest to survive." He knew that either he must remove that burden himself, or others would do it.

Resistance to the legal process, faith in the President, and contempt for their opponents characterized Nixon's inner circle almost to the end. Preventing the "death of a thousand cuts" seemed to be the rallying cry for the President's men. [Chief of Staff Alexander] Haig complained, however, that to some White House aides the slogan meant that Nixon should resign rather than suffer such a painful ordeal—the "pussy fire group," he contemptuously called them, comparing them to Vietnamese who would not stand and fight. Some in the White House felt besieged: "It was us against the world." Every day, it seemed, brought what [Special Assistant to the president] Stephen Bull called the "Oh, Shit Syndrome," meaning another revelation, another disclosure, another indictment. Some left, "either under handcuffs, [or] running for the hills," another aide recalled. But some, like Bull, believed the President would extricate himself—until Bull learned of the June 23 tape.

Still, Bull knew that the White House atmosphere was different; "things just were not happening," he recalled, and the blank pages of the presidential logs offer mute testimony to that fact. For some, like Richard Moore, there was now little to do aside from "long lunch hours." For Moore, it was a time of fear that his friends would go to prison or that he himself would be indicted. Others, like Alan Greenspan, saw the final days as a time to help the President, and, more important, as a time to serve the republic. Greenspan had consistently rejected offers of Administration positions, but near the end he became Chairman of the Council of Economic Advisers, fearing that "the normal process of government would deteriorate or even collapse" unless firm action were taken. Such advisers as Leonard Garment were "amazed" that the President continued to function as well as he did. Nixon, he remembered, "took it right to the end." Finally, for the President's family, of course, it was a mournful time, all the more difficult, apparently, because he could not bring himself to discuss the situation with them. "We never sat down as a family to talk about Watergate," Julie Eisenhower [Nixon's daughter] wrote. For Nixon himself, it was a "nightmare" time.

The President Decides to Resign

Richard Nixon should be taken at his word. When he learned that Republicans and Southern Democrats had banded together to support impeachment, he knew he could not finish his second term. Thereafter, the only question concerned the manner of his leaving. He later wrote that he decided to resign just before the Judiciary Committee voted, meaning, of course, that his talk to his Cabinet on August 6 was pure sham. Other accounts suggest greater uncertainty in his decision. In these versions, Haig is a hero of sorts, a man who kept the President on the course of resignation, sparing the nation more agony. Haig himself may have been the source of such tales; John Mitchell thought that Haig need not write any account of Watergate: "Haig has already gilded the history. I don't think he has to write any more." Such accounts add a measure of drama, to be sure; yet they betray the history of a man who measured his career by a careful calculation of what was best for him. In all probability, Richard Nixon needed little push from others.

The President may have heard a favorable signal on August 7, when Robert McClory told the White House congressional-

Richard Nixon leaves the White House on August 9, 1974, after his resignation from the presidency.

liaison man that [House Judiciary Committee chairman] Rodino had asked him to communicate his view that he had "absolutely no interest in pursuing any kind of criminal action against the President should he elect to resign." According to McClory, Rodino promised to end the impeachment inquiry as well if Nixon stepped down. Speaker Carl Albert concurred, although he added that he had no influence over the Special Prosecutor's course of action. The news from McClory undoubtedly had some appeal. If Nixon learned of that development, then he would have done so just prior to his meeting with [Republican Party leaders] Goldwater, Rhodes, and Scott. That conversation, taken together with the news from Rodino, might well have been influential. Rodino later proved to be as good as his word: he promptly closed down the inquiry after the resignation. Democrats were off the hook of carrying out the formal, irrevocable act of impeachment; moreover, any further action on their part would have reeked of vindictiveness and easily generated a counter-reaction of sympathy for the fallen President.

That evening Nixon began to work in earnest on his resignation speech and arranged to meet Vice President Ford the next day to discuss a transition. In that meeting, the President recommended that Ford retain Haig; the rest of the meeting was awkward, as both men seemed to understand, yet were unable to express, what was required of each.

The following night, Nixon saw more than forty longtime, steadfast supporters. "I just hope I haven't let you down," he told them. But he said later that he knew he had—as he had "let down the country . . . our system of government and the dreams of all those young people that ought to get into government. . . . I . . . let the American people down, and I have to carry that burden with me for the rest of my life." Earlier, he met with congressional leaders from both parties. He told them what he would say to the nation that evening: he had "lost his base" in Congress, and he believed the outcome of the impeachment process to be inevitable. Speaker Albert best remembered that Nixon never discussed the question of whether he had done wrong. Perhaps that was asking too much. Instead, the President broke down in tears.

Nixon's last full day in office proceeded routinely. He vetoed annual appropriations bills for the Agriculture Department and the Environmental Protection Agency on the grounds that they were inflationary. On a lesser, but far more symbolic note, he nominated a judge to fill a federal court seat in Wisconsin which had been vacant for three years. Nixon had sought unsuccessfully to appoint an old friend, Republican Representative Glenn Davis, but the American Bar Association, as well as state groups, had mounted an intense campaign in opposition. The new appointment on August 8 painfully measured the President's decline and powerlessness.

Later that day, Nixon addressed his simple letter of resignation to the keeper of the seals, the Secretary of State: "I hereby resign the Office of President of the United States.". . .

Nixon's Last Day as President

The President spent the afternoon of August 8 correcting and memorizing his resignation speech, to be broadcast that evening. "One thing, Ron, old boy," he feebly joked to [Press Secretary Ron] Ziegler, "we won't have to have any more press conferences, and we won't even have to tell them that, either!" Of course, he had said a similar thing a dozen years earlier in California. He also said that he looked forward to writing, noting that it might be done in prison. "Some of the best writing in history has been done in prison. Think of Lenin and Gandhi," he said.

At 9:00 P.M. the thirty-seventh President addressed the nation from the White House for the thirty-seventh time. Comparatively little of his talk had to do with Watergate and his resignation. If Richard Nixon were indeed to write from prison, first he would broadcast his own apologia. Watergate had been "a long and difficult period." He wished to carry on and persevere in the presidency, but events of the past few days convinced him that "I no longer have a strong enough political base in the Congress to justify continuing that effort." He wanted to "see the constitutional process through," but with the loss of his political base, he said, the process had been served, and there was no need to prolong it. Because of the Watergate situation, he contended, Congress would not give him the necessary support to govern effectively. With a hint of defiance, he asserted that he had never been a quitter. To resign was "abhorrent to every instinct" within him. But he would put "the interests of America first." America, he said, needed a full-time President and a full-time Congress; an impeachment battle would only drain both the institutions and the nation. "Therefore, I shall resign the Presidency effective at noon tomorrow," he added.

Nixon seemed sincere as he expressed hope that his act would heal the nation's wounds. And he offered what apparently he had not told the congressional leaders who had conferred with him: "I regret deeply any injuries that may have been done in the course of the events that led to this decision. I would say only that if some of my judgments were wrong—and some were wrong—they were made in what I believed at the time to be the best interest of the Nation." It was Richard Nixon's only moment that approximated contrition.

The rest of the talk focused on his achievements—the end of the Vietnam war, the opening to China, the conciliatory responses of the Arab nations to his diplomatic efforts, and the agreements with the Soviet Union. Nothing was said of any gains toward that domestic peace which Nixon had promised more than five years earlier. Finally, he insisted that resignation would not be his St. Helena; rather, he promised that the nation would see more of him in the years to come.

The networks followed the President's resignation speech with the "instant analysis" that Nixon and Agnew had so bitterly assailed. Nixon undoubtedly savored the irony. Now, the commentators treated him generously—"a touch of class," "conciliatory," "few things in his presidency became him as much as his manner of leaving." He also would have heard more familiar chords. One commentator remarked: "From the viewpoint of Congress, that wasn't a very satisfactory speech." Nixon had expressed "regret," to be sure; but finally, the reason he gave for resigning was that Congress had deprived him of a "political base," making it impossible for him to continue in office. It was the opening salvo in his campaign for history.

Six years earlier, to the day, Nixon had delivered perhaps the best speech of his career as he accepted the Republican presidential nomination. He had told the nation that he would restore respect for the law. "Time is running out," he said at that time, "for the merchants of crime and corruption in American society."

Nixon's Departure from the White House

The morning after his resignation announcement, the President gave another speech, a "spontaneous thing," he called it, as he spoke in the East Room of the White House to an assembled group of White House and Administration workers. As often before in his career, Nixon was anxious to bare his soul—never more so than in this, his darkest hour, and perhaps the darkest hour of the American presidency. But it was the wrong time. Now, the time was more appropriate for a quiet fade-out—unless he had another goal in mind. Perhaps he did. The Friday morning talk marked the flip side of the speech the night before—different words, yet all part of the same album designed to impress indelibly the image of Richard Nixon as a man grievously wronged and a man not about to leave the public stage forever. It was, he said, "a beginning."

In the open society of America, the most private of moments often become the most public of spectacles. When a president embraces his family, visits the Lincoln Memorial, or receives a foreign visitor, we know the probing eye of the television camera will accompany him not only to give us "news," but to allow us vicariously to experience the event itself. Richard Nixon's last appearance before White House workers and Administration loyalists seemed, by its nature, a private event. The President could have conducted it in private, had he preferred. His family, he admitted, protested that "after all the agony television had caused us, its prying eye should [not] be allowed to intrude on this last and most intimate moment of all." But he sensed an opportunity to serve himself and seized the moment. "That's the way it has to be," he told them, adding that he owed it to his supporters and to the people. His daughter dutifully found her name mark on the floor. Clearly, Nixon would persist in his unceasing quest for gaining love and understanding from America. Spontaneous? In all likelihood, the occasion had all the spontaneity of a pointillist painting.

Nixon had home adversity through the years, sometimes with grace, other times with petulance, but always with verve. As he prepared to depart from office, he was reconciled to the inevitability of his punishment. The moment presented him with the opportunity to display a rarely seen introspective side of himself. Whether wallowing in the banality of self-pity or reciting his achievements with a feisty grit and pride, he remained a compelling phenomenon to admirers and adversaries alike.

President Richard Nixon Announces the Watergate Investigation

by Richard M. Nixon

President Richard M. Nixon made history as the first American president to resign from the office. His decision came in the wake of a scandal that shook the nation socially, politically, and constitutionally.

Nixon was born on January 9, 1913, in Yorba Linda, California. After completing law school at Duke University, he returned to California to practice law until he joined the navy in 1942. After World War II he set his sights on a political career. In his 1946 campaign for Congress he cast suspicions of Communist sympathies on his opponent. In fact, intolerance for communism characterized much of his political career. He won the race and four years later won a seat in the Senate. Only two years later, Nixon was Dwight D. Eisenhower's running mate in the presidential election. A popular war hero, Eisenhower easily won, and Nixon was initiated into the White House. In his new position, Nixon focused his efforts on foreign policy, a forum where he could advance anticommunism. Although he was the favored presidential candidate in 1960, he lost to John F. Kennedy.

After a failed gubernatorial campaign in California, Nixon settled

---

Richard M. Nixon, televised address, Washington, April 30, 1973.

back into practicing law while rebuilding his political career. In 1968 he won the presidential election. A major element of his campaign was his promise to end the Vietnam War. Although he offered no details of his plan, Americans' readiness to get out of Vietnam made them responsive. After years of continued violence, a peace treaty was finally signed in 1973, and American troops returned home. But Nixon's 1972 reelection was soon tainted by emerging information about Watergate. The scandal would ultimately bring Nixon's administration to its knees and force the president to resign his office rather than face impeachment. Nixon initially proclaimed innocence in the following speech to the American public. His words here would later deal a blow to his credibility.

Good evening:

I want to talk to you tonight from my heart on a subject of deep concern to every American.

In recent months, members of my Administration and officials of the Committee for the Re-Election of the President—including some of my closest friends and most trusted aides—have been charged with involvement in what has come to be known as the Watergate affair. These include charges of illegal activity during and preceding the 1972 Presidential election and charges that responsible officials participated in efforts to cover up that illegal activity.

The inevitable result of these charges has been to raise serious questions about the integrity of the White House itself. Tonight I wish to address those questions.

Nixon Receives Word of Watergate Break-in

Last June 17, while I was in Florida trying to get a few days rest after my visit to Moscow, I first learned from news reports of the Watergate break-in. I was appalled at this senseless, illegal action, and I was shocked to learn that employees of the Re-Election Committee were apparently among those guilty. I immediately ordered an investigation by appropriate Government authorities. On September 15, as you will recall, indictments were brought against seven defendants in the case.

As the investigations went forward, I repeatedly asked those conducting the investigation whether there was any reason to believe that members of my Administration were in any way involved. I received repeated assurances that there were not. Because of these continuing reassurances, because I believed the reports I was getting, because I had faith in the persons from whom I was getting them, I discounted the stories in the press that appeared to implicate members of my Administration or other officials of the campaign committee.

Until March of this year, I remained convinced that the denials were true and that the charges of involvement by members of the White House Staff were false. The comments I made during this period, and the comments made by my Press Secretary in my behalf, were based on the information provided to us at the time we made those comments. However, new information then came to me which persuaded me that there was a real possibility that some of these charges were true, and suggesting further that there had been an effort to conceal the facts both from the public, from you, and from me.

As a result, on March 21, I personally assumed the responsibility for coordinating intensive new inquiries into the matter, and I personally ordered those conducting the investigations to get all the facts and to report them directly to me, right here in this office. . . .

Nixon Had Delegated Campaign Responsibilities

Looking back at the history of this case, two questions arise:

How could it have happened?

Who is to blame?

Political commentators have correctly observed that during my 27 years in politics I have always previously insisted on running my own campaigns for office.

But 1972 presented a very different situation. In both domestic and foreign policy, 1972 was a year of crucially important decisions, of intense negotiations, of vital new directions, particularly in working toward the goal which has been my overriding concern throughout my political career—the goal of bringing peace to America, peace to the world.

That is why I decided, as the 1972 campaign approached, that the Presidency should come first and politics second. To the maximum extent possible, therefore, I sought to delegate campaign operations to remove the day-to-day campaign decisions from the President's office and from the White House. I also, as you recall, severely limited the number of my own campaign appearances.

Who, then, is to blame for what happened in this case?

For specific criminal actions by specific individuals, those who committed those actions must, of course, bear the liability and pay the penalty.

Nixon Accepts Blame

For the fact that alleged improper actions took place within the White House or within my campaign organization, the easiest course would be for me to blame those to whom I delegated the responsibility to run the campaign. But that would be a cowardly thing to do.

I will not place the blame on subordinates—on people whose zeal exceeded their judgment and who may have done wrong in a cause they deeply believed to be right.

In any organization, the man at the top must bear the responsibility. That responsibility, therefore, belongs here, in this office. I accept it. And I pledge to you tonight, from this office, that I will do everything in my power to ensure that the guilty are brought to justice and that such abuses are purged from our political processes in the years to come, long after I have left this office.

This Incident Gives Hope to Political Process

Some people, quite properly appalled at the abuses that occurred, will say that Watergate demonstrates the bankruptcy of the American political system. I believe precisely the opposite is true. Watergate represented a series of illegal acts and bad judgments by a number of individuals. It was the system that has brought the facts to light and that will bring those guilty to justice—a system that in this case has included a determined grand jury, honest prosecutors, a courageous judge, John Sirica, and a vigorous free press.

It is essential now that we place our faith in that system—and especially in the judicial system. It is essential that we let the judicial process go forward, respecting those safeguards that are established to protect the innocent as well as to convict the guilty. It is essential that in reacting to the excesses of others, we not fall into excesses ourselves. . . .

Return Focus to America as a Whole

There is also vital work to be done right here in America: to ensure prosperity, and that means a good job for everyone who wants to work; to control inflation, that I know worries every housewife, everyone who tries to balance a family budget in America; to set in motion new and better ways of ensuring progress toward a better life for all Americans.

When I think of this office—of what it means—I think of all

On August 8, 1974, Richard Nixon formally resigned as president of the United States. Here, he gives his farewell speech to the White House staff.

the things that I want to accomplish for this Nation, of all the things I want to accomplish for you.

On Christmas Eve, during my terrible personal ordeal of the renewed bombing of North Vietnam, which after 12 years of war finally helped to bring America peace with honor, I sat down just before midnight. I wrote out some of my goals for my second term as President.

Let me read them to you.

"To make it possible for our children, and for our children's children, to live in a world of peace.

"To make this country be more than ever a land of opportunity—of equal opportunity, full opportunity for every American.

"To provide jobs for all who can work, and generous help for those who cannot work.

"To establish a climate of decency and civility, in which each person respects the feelings and the dignity and the God-given rights of his neighbor.

"To make this a land in which each person can dare to dream, can live his dreams—not in fear, but in hope—proud of his community, proud of his country, proud of what America has meant to himself and to the world."

These are great goals. I believe we can, we must work for them. We can achieve them. But we cannot achieve these goals unless we dedicate ourselves to another goal.

Restoring American Politics Is of Utmost Importance

We must maintain the integrity of the White House, and that integrity must be real, not transparent. There can be no whitewash at the White House.

We must reform our political process—ridding it not only of the violations of the law but also of the ugly mob violence and other inexcusable campaign tactics that have been too often practiced and too readily accepted in the past, including those that may have been a response by one side to the excesses or expected excesses of the other side. Two wrongs do not make a right.

I have been in public life for more than a quarter of a century. Like any other calling, politics has good people and bad people. And let me tell you, the great majority in politics—in the Congress, in the Federal Government, in the State government—are good people. I know that it can be very easy, under the intensive pressures of a campaign, for even well-intentioned people to fall into shady tactics—to rationalize this on the grounds that what is at stake is of such importance to the Nation that the end justifies the means. And both of our great parties have been guilty of such tactics in the past.

In recent years, however, the campaign excesses that have occurred on all sides have provided a sobering demonstration of how far this false doctrine can take us. The lesson is clear: America, in its political campaigns, must not again fall into the trap of letting the end, however great that end is, justify the means.

I urge the leaders of both political parties, I urge citizens, all of you, everywhere, to join in working toward a new set of standards, new rules and procedures to ensure that future elections will be as nearly free of such abuses as they possibly can be made. This is my goal. I ask you to join in making it America's goal.

Nixon's High Hopes for Remainder of Term

When I was inaugurated for a second time this past January 20, I gave each member of my Cabinet and each member of my senior White House Staff a special 4-year calendar, with each day marked to show the number of days remaining to the Administration. In the inscription on each calendar, I wrote these words: "The Presidential term which begins today consists of 1,461 days—no more, no less. Each can be a day of strengthening and renewal for America; each can add depth and dimension to the American experience. If we strive together, if we make the most of the challenge and the opportunity that these days offer us, they can stand out as great days for America, and great moments in the history of the world."

I looked at my own calendar this morning up at Camp David as I was working on this speech. It showed exactly 1,361 days remaining in my term. I want these to be the best days in America's history, because I love America. I deeply believe that America is the hope of the world. And I know that in the quality and wisdom of the leadership America gives lies the only hope for millions of people all over the world that they can live their lives in peace and freedom. We must be worthy of that hope, in every sense of the word. Tonight, I ask for your prayers to help me in everything that I do throughout the days of my Presidency to be worthy of their hopes and of yours.

God bless America and God bless each and every one of you.

The Fall of Saigon and Assessing U.S. Involvement in the Vietnam War

by Robert D. Schulzinger

The Vietnam War raged on in faraway Asia, but it also took a toll in the United States. It was an unpopular war, and one that inspired numerous protests, many of which turned violent. The Vietnam War was significant socially, politically, and culturally. It is also one of the least understood military efforts in American history.

After World War II Vietnam was still part of French Indochina, but the United States was concerned about it because of the potential spread of communism. When Communist North Korea invaded South Korea in 1950, President Harry S. Truman was alarmed and knew he had to make a decisive move. It appeared that Communist forces in Asia were on the move. In 1954 the Viet Minh drove the ruling French out and became independent. As a result, the country was partitioned. For South Vietnam to withstand the attacks that were sure to keep coming from North Vietnam, however, it needed American support. At first the United States provided nonmilitary support, but eventually American troops arrived on South Vietnamese soil. In 1964 President Lyndon B. Johnson passed the Gulf of Tonkin Resolution, empowering him to use his discretion and authority in the Vietnam matter. The American military presence grew, and in 1967 the number of troops reached five hundred thousand.

Robert D. Schulzinger, *A Time for War: The United States and Vietnam, 1941–1975*. New York: Oxford University Press, 1997. Copyright © 1997 by Oxford University Press, Inc. Reproduced by permission.

Vocal opposition to the war was increasingly common at home. At first citizen protesters composed the bulk of the antiwar movement, but by the end of the 1960s, top government officials stopped supporting the war. In 1968 Richard Nixon was elected and he promised to end the war. Once in office Nixon's plan was to provide arms and resources to South Vietnam but gradually withdraw troops. Still, the war thundered on as peace talks proceeded very slowly. In 1973 a cease-fire went into effect, and American troops (including prisoners of war) returned home. Although this was good for the Americans, it sealed the fate of South Vietnam, whose capital city of Saigon fell to the Communist Vietcong in April 1975.

At the time of the war, and still today, the events and decisions surrounding the Vietnam War prompted passionate debate about foreign policy, containment, international politics, the proper use of military force, and political ideologies. Whereas some critics claim that the United States had no business getting involved at all, commentators on the other end of the spectrum maintain that the U.S. failure was in not committing wholly.

In the following excerpt Robert D. Schulzinger reviews the events of the last days of the Vietnam War. Schulzinger is a professor of history and international studies who has written numerous books on diplomacy and international affairs.

On April 4 [1975] Army Chief of Staff Frederick Weyand provided one of the gloomiest assessments of the military situation in Vietnam. [President Gerald] Ford had earlier dispatched his fact-finding mission with the admonition, "You are not going over to lose." But Weyand returned from a one-week visit to South Vietnam to report that "the Government of Vietnam is on the brink of a total military defeat." They were certain to go down if aid was not increased. Even if it were, he thought that the chance for their survival "marginal at best." He also scotched an idea floated by General William C. Westmoreland, the former commander in Vietnam, for renewed U.S. air strikes over the North. Weyand realized that Congress would forbid any air action over the North. He did propose, however, that Ford consider the use of troops to help the evacuation of the remaining six thousand U.S. personnel and some ten thousand South Vietnamese tied to the Americans. The madcap evacuation of Da Nang convinced Weyand that the United States needed to provide protection when Saigon fell.

A few days later, on April 9, CIA Director [William] Colby reinforced Weyand's grave assessment. The day before, a dissident officer of the South Vietnamese air force had used his F-5 fighter jet to bomb the presidential palace. He then flew the plane into communist-controlled territory and defected to the PRG [Provisional Revolutionary Government of South Vietnam] with denunciations of Thieu [president of the Republic of Vietnam] and the Americans. Thieu then tried to reorganize his government to bring in opposition leaders, but most of them were reluctant to join such an obviously lost cause. Any new government would probably only negotiate terms with the communists. Colby believed that, for its part, Hanoi "is not interested in a compromise but rather in a figleaf for a North Vietnamese takeover under military pressure."

Military Presence No Longer Effective

Faced with an impossible military situation, Ford agreed with [press secretary Ron] Nessen and his other political advisers that a continuation of the war was the last thing the American public wanted. It was hardly a close call. Throughout the sixty days preceding the fall of Saigon, the White House had found widespread disapproval whenever it measured congressional and public attitudes toward a continuation of military aid to Saigon. Phnom Penh fell to the Khmer Rouge [insurgent Cambodian Communists] at the beginning of April. The collapse of the Cambodian armed forces infected the South Vietnamese soldiers. U.S. military intelligence in South Vietnam believed that "Saigon can hold out only a few weeks. . . . Barring massive U.S. intervention or a deliberate North Vietnamese pause it is going to go." Public opinion in the United States opposed such intervention. Illinois Republican Robert Michel reported that his constituents believed that the reluctance of the South Vietnamese armed forces to fight meant that "we can only provide humanitarian assistance."

For the rest of April, Congress would only consider providing such humanitarian assistance. Ford addressed Congress on April 10 to ask for the additional $300 million in military aid, but there was little likelihood lawmakers would approve. Four days later, he met with the Senate Committee on Foreign Relations at the White House. Both Republicans and Democrats told him that the war was over. As Senator Howard Baker (R., Tenn.) put it, "An evacuation of the American citizens [is] so urgent that everything else—legality, Thieu's incumbency, everything else—[is] secondary to that." Other members of Congress told the White House that only humanitarian assistance was possible. Representative Bella Abzug (D., N.Y.), one of the most vociferous critics of U.S. involvement in the war, called for an end to military assistance to the government of President Nguyen Van Thieu, but she said that "the human suffering and chaos in South Vietnam require prompt humanitarian and constructive action by the U.S. government, whose wrong policies and illegal intervention for the past decade are largely responsible for the current tragic plight of the South Vietnamese." Senator Walter Mondale (D., Minn.), who had expressed growing opposition to U.S. involvement in Vietnam over the previous four years, agreed that Congress would not provide military assistance but would be moved by the plight of Vietnamese children, who were the "innocent victims of the conflict."

Even as Ford acknowledged the end of the South's ability to

The Vietnam War resulted in the devastation of homes and entire villages. Here, women salvage belongings after a Vietcong attack.

defend itself, Graham Martin [U.S. Ambassador to South Vietnam] employed a bewildering array of tactics, some at war with one another, to persuade some foreign power to come to the aid of the South Vietnamese. He flattered [Henry] Kissinger for his speeches favoring additional aid to South Vietnam. He told the Secretary of State that he was like George Marshall advocating aid to Western Europe at the beginning of the Cold War—indeed, he was a "genius." Martin also thought it might help to obtain aid for South Vietnam by aligning himself with Kissinger against professional Foreign Service officers who opposed aid. These people took "great care to insure their intellectual hemlines are not one silly milimeter [sic] above or below the current conventional intellectual mode."

When it became clear to Martin that Congress would not approve additional aid, the Ambassador looked to other countries. He persisted in a yearlong effort to have Saudi Arabia underwrite Saigon's war effort. He cabled the U.S. embassy in Jidda, Saudi Arabia, that South Vietnam was now a "victim of a concerted propaganda campaign of distortion in the U.S. . . . fanned by the same elements of media which are so vocal in support of Israel." Despite the visit of a South Vietnamese representative to Saudi Arabia, the Saudis declined to back an obviously losing cause.

While Martin desperately sought military aid for South Vietnam, he resisted efforts at humanitarian assistance, fearing such aid would convince the government of South Vietnam that U.S. officials had concluded their cause was hopeless. For the same reason, Martin resisted for as long as possible the evacuation of U.S. personnel, their dependents, and South Vietnamese who worked for the United States.

Political Posturing

The differences of opinion among Ford, his political advisers, Kissinger, and Martin about the appropriate course for the United States to follow in South Vietnam demonstrated that Vietnam still mattered at the upper levels of the U.S. government in 1975, but the issue no longer engaged the public the way it once had done. Now the major public concern was to avoid discussion of Vietnam. Such widespread revulsion helps understand why Ford chose to suppress discussion of the promises made by Richard Nixon to President Thieu at the time of the Paris agreements to provide military assistance to South Vietnam should the North violate the agreements. Once the existence of the letters from Nixon to Thieu became known in 1975, Ford's critics contended that he should have fully disclosed the contents of the letters to Congress at the time of the final debate over providing aid to South Vietnam.

Given Kissinger's general opposition to sharing confidential information with Congress, there was little likelihood that Ford would have turned the documents over to lawmakers. Having overruled Kissinger on a substantial matter—making an all-out push for aid to South Vietnam—Ford had little incentive to further irritate his Secretary of State by turning over documents to a hostile Congress. Furthermore, it is hard to believe that anything, including the disclosure of these promises, would have altered the general public aversion to re-entering the war.

Meanwhile, North Vietnamese forces approached Saigon. Thieu's domestic opponents from the right, led by former Vice President Nguyen Cao Ky, to the neutralists, led by General Duong Van Minh, all wanted Thieu to leave. Even Ambassador Martin, his most steadfast supporter, believed that a new government might be able to work out an arrangement with the advancing communist forces to avoid a surrender of the city. On April 21 President Thieu finally resigned the presidency. Vice President Tran Van Huong replaced him. Thieu spoke on television to the nation that evening, seeking the vindication of history. He explained that he had always opposed the Paris agreements because it legitimized the Vietcong. He said that U.S. aid had been critical in blunting the communist attacks during Tet in 1968 and in the spring of 1972. Now that the United States could no longer be counted on to provide military aid, Thieu said he had no choice. He blamed Kissinger for not making good on Nixon's commitment to supply new military aid if the North violated the Paris agreements and angrily refused Kissinger's offer of asylum in the United States.

Ford Announces War's End Before the War Ends

Finally, on April 23, Ford received wild applause from six thousand young people in the audience at Tulane University and praise from political and foreign affairs analysts around the country when he announced that "the war in Vietnam is over as far as America is concerned." After Ford spoke, he pointedly informed the press that he reached the decision on his own, without consulting Kissinger, whose high reputation for foreign policy achievement had recently seemed to overshadow Ford's. The President was elated by the warm reception of his speech. Most Americans seemed relieved that the war had ended.

But it had not. An unnatural calm hung over Saigon for the next few days. North Vietnamese and Vietcong tanks were on the outskirts of the city, but refrained from entering. In both Saigon and Washington, American officials delayed orders to evacuate Saigon for as long as possible. Ever the blind optimist, Martin thought that Saigon could hold out for another few weeks if the United States did not force a panic by withdrawal. As Ford told the National Security Council on April 24, "I think it is very important to stay there as long as we can contribute, to evacuate in a way that will not promote panic." Until the end, Kissinger tried to enlist the Soviet Union to help the Americans out of a jam in Vietnam. This time he wanted them to arrange a lull in the fighting to permit U.S. personnel to leave peacefully.

By now, events in Vietnam were more out of Soviet hands than ever. On April 27 President Huong resigned and was replaced by General Duong Van Minh. The war had come full circle. Minh, of course, had led the coup against Ngo Dinh Diem [the first president of the Republic of South Vietnam] on November 1963. A presumed neutralist, he had been ousted himself by the Americans in January 1964. In 1967 Thieu had banned his participation in the presidential elections. Now Minh was president, trying to arrange a peaceful accommodation with the triumphant communists. He offered them a cease-fire but they refused.

Final Battle for Saigon

On April 28 the final battle for Saigon began with North Vietnamese and Vietcong artillery attacks on Tansonnhut Airport. The shelling killed two U.S. marines helping to evacuate civilians and rendered all but one runway useless. On the morning of April 28, Kissinger met with the Washington Special Actions Group to decide what to do if Tansonnhut were to be closed. If that happened "we should pull out all the Americans" by helicopter from Saigon.

That evening Ford and his principal foreign policy and military advisers made the fateful decision to evacuate the U.S. embassy. Secretary of Defense James Schlesinger opposed using

American air power to cover the departure. There were four thousand North Vietnamese sappers in the capital, he said. "They will attack the embassy if we attack by fire." The NSC [National Security Council] meeting also agreed with Kissinger to save the Americans before helping the South Vietnamese who depended on them. "If we have to go out, priority will go to the Americans," he said.

Chaos in Evacuating the City

On the morning of April 29 more than ten thousand Vietnamese who depended on the Americans surrounded the grounds of the U.S. embassy. They pushed papers that they thought authorized them passage out of the city onto the marine guards, who had orders not to let Vietnamese pass. About four thousand climbed over the walls and forced their way through the gates. "Can someone tell me what the hell is going on!" Kissinger exploded when he heard reports that Vietnamese had boarded helicopters leaving the roof of the embassy. "The orders are that only Americans are to be evacuated." But the Vietnamese would not let the nearly six hundred Americans remaining in Vietnam leave unless some of the Vietnamese went, too.

The evacuation was also slowed by Martin's foot-dragging. The ambassador wanted Americans to stay until the very last minute to give heart to the Vietnamese. His delays infuriated General George Brown, Chairman of the Joint Chiefs of Staff. "The ambassador has got to get those people out of there. Can't you tell him to get them out of there?" he asked Kissinger. "Those are his bloody orders, goddammit!" Kissinger shouted. Exhausted, angry, fed up with Martin and the war, Kissinger explained, "Yes, I'll instruct the Ambassador to get those people out, but he's been ordered to get those people out a hundred times." Finally, Martin led the last of the Americans up the ladder of a helicopter on the roof of the U.S. embassy for evacuation to aircraft carriers waiting off the coast. In the end, about 5,000 people, including 4,100 Vietnamese and 900 Americans, were evacuated from the roof of the embassy on April 29. Americans also ordered the South Vietnamese air force to land their helicopters on American ships to keep them from falling into the hands of the North Vietnamese. A few South Vietnamese pilots flew their crafts to the American vessels under the impression that they would refuel, regroup and rejoin the fighting. But when they landed marines told them, "Stand back, boys. The war is over." The Americans then pushed the craft into the sea.

Kissinger Predicts Disaster in Vietnam

On April 30 a somber and angry Henry Kissinger predicted a catastrophic political aftermath for the country in general and for Ford in particular. Hours after television pictures flashed around the world showing the mad evacuation of the last U.S. civilians from the roof of the American embassy in Saigon, Kissinger took stock of the debacle in a speech in the East Room of the White House. He warned the assembled high officials that the United States would "pay a price for what happened in Southeast Asia." The United States would be tested by its adversaries over the next few months. He wondered whether the American public might not grow despondent at the burdens of leadership in international affairs. Yet he predicted a resurrection of firmness in U.S. foreign policy. Adversaries who celebrated America's discomfiture were "doing so prematurely." Angry and frustrated that his handiwork at the Paris negotiations had gone so publicly sour, Kissinger pointed the finger of blame at the top. Politicians basking in the glow of public approval for having ended U.S. participation in the war should reflect on the fate of British Prime Minister Neville Chamberlain. He was "the most popular man in England in 1938 [at the time of the Munich agreement]—eighteen months later he was finished."

How fitting that the first post-mortem on the war by an American Secretary of State revived the memory of Munich. From the very beginning, U.S. policy in Vietnam had been linked to the analogy of the moral failing of the Western powers in appeasing Hitler's limitless ambitions. The comparison never fit reality but even at the very end Americans were not thinking about the country they were supposed to be helping. As always, they were preoccupied with something—be it domestic politics, containment, the Cold War, or credibility—other than what was actually happening in Vietnam. . . .

The War in Retrospect

So, was the war in Vietnam worth it—for the Americans or the Vietnamese? The immediate response is: Of course not. Vietnam was unified; the nationalists/revolutionaries won. But the cost included three million dead, as many as fifteen million made refugees at different times throughout the war, horrible physical devastation, over one million people, including some of the most industrious and educated, forced to flee, and the creation of one of the world's poorest economies. Despite the fears expressed by American officials, Vietnam did not endure a bloodbath after the communist triumph, but the victors did impose an authoritarian, repressive regime. Much of the death and damage was the responsibility of the United States. The victorious revolutionaries bore responsibility for the forced departure of the refugees, the terrible economic mismanagement, and the political repression of postwar Vietnam.

Was the war worth it for the United States? Again, of course, the predominant answer is no. There were fifty-eight thousand dead and far more severely wounded than in earlier wars (primarily because of the improvements in medical evacuation.) The U.S. economy suffered years of inflation because of government policies pursued during the Vietnam years. In the aftermath of the Cold War, it is also hard to see that the investment in Vietnam had anything much to do with the demise of the Soviet Union. The most enduring legacy of all, perhaps, was a persistent distrust of public institutions and the officials who ran them.

But the United States emerged stronger than many people expected from the crucible of Vietnam. The recriminations over the war never reached the level of the debate in Weimar Germany over responsibility for Germany's defeat in World War I, despite fears expressed in 1975 that they would. While both Dan Quayle, the successful vice presidential candidate in 1988, who had been a hawk, and Bill Clinton, the victorious presidential candidate in 1992, who had been a dove, generated furious opposition for avoiding the draft, both won their elections.

Ironies abound. The public institution that learned the lessons of the Vietnam war best was the military. Its reputation by the mid-1970s had reached its nadir: within the following two decades it became one of the most highly esteemed organizations in the United States. Moreover, the five hundred thousand Vietnamese and other Southeast Asians who came to the United States after 1975 became one of the country's greatest human resources.

Finally, the prevalent hostility and skepticism—some people characterize it as cynicism—Americans express toward their leaders and their public institutions is partly a consequence of the war in Vietnam. An old anti-war slogan—"I love my country but fear my government"—reverberates. The coarsening of political discourse during the past generation has some of its roots in the agony of U.S. involvement in Vietnam. But the positive side of this distrust of public institutions and officials is a deeply felt desire for accountability and responsiveness, and a willingness to use the influence of the media, the courts, and the government to meet popular needs. The United States is a louder place now. It is a more diverse society, with fewer enforced norms. It is also, surprisingly, a more democratic place, in large measure because the country went through the agonizing experience of Vietnam.

A Top Political Figure of the Republic of South Vietnam Recalls the Fall of Saigon

by Nguyen Cao Ky

The following excerpt is from a memoir by Nguyen Cao Ky, who was Vietnam's prime minister from 1965 to 1967 and its vice president from 1967 to 1971. His love of his country and his political insights renders this an important document in understanding what it was like to be in Saigon when it fell to the Communist Vietcong in April 1975.

As a young man, Ky joined the military and distinguished himself. Because of his abilities and his French wife (Vietnam was part of French Indochina at the time), Ky was able to move quickly up the military hierarchy. He participated in a coup against nationalist leader Ngo Dinh Diem in 1963 and another one against General Duong Van "Big" Minh in 1964. His courage and leadership won him a position as head of the air force later in 1964. Through a series of military and political maneuvers, Ky became prime minister in 1965. He ascended to this position partly because the United States, now a major presence in Vietnam, supported him. As prime minister, Ky worked closely with American ambassadors and military leaders.

Nguyen Cao Ky, *Twenty Years and Twenty Days*. New York: Stein and Day, 1976. Copyright © 1976 by Stein and Day. Reproduced by permission.

When elections were held in 1967, Ky participated in manipulating the results so that he would be the new vice president and General Nguyen Van Thieu would be president. The relationship between the two men quickly soured, however, when Thieu was accused of commanding the devastating Tet Offensive on South Vietnam. Lacking support, Ky retired from politics in 1971, but he stayed in the public eye. His commitment to preserving his country from communism was evident when, just prior to Saigon's fall in 1975, he organized a protest in front of the American embassy, declaring he would never leave Vietnam. When Saigon fell, however, he left with the Americans but vowed to return to fight communism in his native land. As of the late 1990s, Ky was working in the United States.

W e had shelved the idea of a coup to depose President Thieu, trusting the American ambassador, but as the hours ticked by, our first nagging impatience for action began to turn into qualms of doubt. My "hot line" telephone to the American embassy had become strangely silent. The daily phone calls from [Major General Charles] Timmes [of the U.S. Military Assistance Advisory Group]—always so friendly, always so encouraging—had unaccountably dried up. I came under more and more pressure from my colleagues on the National Salvation Committee to take drastic action. Finally I could delay no longer. I picked up the phone and asked Timmes bluntly, "What's happening?" He was not exactly evasive, but he seemed to hesitate. It is not always easy (or fair) to form a conclusion from a phone talk, but I had the impression that he was embarrassed. "For the moment our hands are tied," he said, "It's very difficult, very delicate. Just hang on until we let you know." It was clear that something funny was going on, especially when I learned that [U.S. ambassador to South Vietnam Graham] Martin's behavior was becoming nothing short of bizarre. More and more he was playing the role of an arrogant Caesar. While Washington urged him to prepare for a full-scale evacuation, he apparently disregarded their orders because he felt that a too-hasty evacuation program would damage the dignity of the United States and his own personal dignity.

How the Americans treated their own people in Saigon was their affair, but there were hundreds of Vietnamese workers on the United States payroll who would be marked for certain death if Saigon fell. They had all been promised a ticket to safety. Martin had boasted, "If Americans have to go. I will take a million Vietnamese with me."

Well, while Washington told him to do just this in cables that he ignored, I could see the result for myself on the air base. Scores of big U.S. transport planes flew in past my windows every day, loaded with precious supplies—but nearly all flew back half empty, when they could have taken a far more precious cargo to safety.

Martin did try to persuade Phan Quang Dan, deputy prime minister, to allow orphans to be evacuated, but this was for propaganda, for Martin wrote in a letter to Dan that "this evacuation . . . will create a shift in American public opinion in favor of Vietnam," explaining that, once in America, the children would appear on TV and "the effect would be tremendous."

In fact Martin was hoping to persuade Congress to reverse its veto on arms aid to Vietnam, and he backed his plan up with a never-ending stream of photographs of atrocities and inspired stories calculated to wring the hearts of American people, at the same time as he was assuring all of us, "Be calm. Saigon is in no danger."

Even more incredible, at this critical moment he ordered embassy officials to compile a detailed study of the Vietnamese government information service. The man was not only stupid. He was mad.

Suddenly contacts inside the government told me on my private grapevine that Thieu was on the point of being ordered to resign. "There's no doubt about it," one told me, "all they're doing now is trying to find a formula to save everyone's face.". . .

Thieu Steps Down

Martin forced Thieu to go, but with some bizarre thought of obeying the laws of protocol, he replaced him with the vice president.

I shall never forget the moment when fifty-two-year-old Thieu told the people of Vietnam that he had been forced out of office. Two hundred friends and followers were jammed in my house to listen to the pathetic hour-long speech by the man Martin had backed, the man who had allowed the Reds to reach the outskirts of the capital. We could hear the gunfire as we listened and watched.

I was ashamed. Ashamed that any Vietnamese leader could behave as Thieu behaved in his speech. Looking at the small TV screen, at Thieu in an open-necked bush shirt, my mind flashed back to the day Johnson agreed to my request to install television in Vietnam. I felt almost sorry we had ever discussed the matter of TV as Thieu started to blame the United States for its lack of resolve. In a tirade against those who had kept him in office, he accused America of not fulfilling its obligations.

Dr. [Henry] Kissinger [national security advisor], he said, had tricked him into signing the Paris peace agreement and had then gone back on his word by refusing to send military aid to South Vietnam. We had lost because the United States failed to re-supply the army and send aid. "You ran away and left us to do the job that you could not do. We have nothing and you want us to achieve where you failed," he accused the Americans angrily. "At the time of the peace agreement the United States agreed to replace equipment on a one-for-one basis. But the United States did not keep its word. Is America's word reliable these days?"

Then came the surprise. Thieu was succeeded by the vice president, seventy-one-year-old Tran Van Huong; dear old Huong, the ex-schoolmaster, who had given me such a handsome wedding gift of 200,000 piastres. By now his eyesight was so bad that he could hardly read. When Huong became president I could only assume that Big Minh [a military and political leader] was waiting in the wings.

Communist Forces Close in on Saigon

There followed a week of terror and confusion. Huong was a nonentity. Nothing was done to stem the onward surge of the enemy. By April 26 the Communists had cut Saigon off from its main source of food, and its only remaining port, Vung Tau, forty-five miles southeast of the capital. Twice they had bombarded the heart of Saigon, as a foretaste of things to come if we did not capitulate. . . .

Big Minh Assumes Presidency

Huong lasted a week as president. Then Martin, having observed the niceties of diplomacy by allowing the vice president to step up (since there had been no election), now felt the time had come to install his protégé, Big Minh. It was decided to replace Huong on April 28, and on the 27th the fifty-nine-year-old Big Minh was

South Vietnamese soldiers such as those pictured above were defeated when the Communist Vietcong took Saigon in 1975.

asking both houses of the National Assembly for their formal approval, when the Communists gave a demonstration of their disapproval—by flying three jets captured from us in the North over the presidential palace, clearly indicating that they were unwilling to talk with Big Minh, but would take Saigon by force.

That was the night I talked to Von Marbod of the American Defense Department and begged him to help us to fight in the Mekong Delta—a request that was refused. The next morning my wife, Mai, and our children left for Honolulu on the last U.S. military plane to leave the base. She had twenty minutes to pack a suitcase after breakfast, and I was not even there to say farewell.

At three o'clock that afternoon the same pilot who had warned me of the assassins who had infiltrated the base on General Quang's orders came in with another piece of startling news. Thieu had, as we knew, bolted, but in the rush to run away he had forgotten all about Quang, his partner in crime.

"Quang's at the headquarters of the General Staff," said the pilot, "and I'm told he's absolutely furious. Thieu promised him a ride, then left without telling him."

A junior officer cried, "Can we go and arrest him, Sir—and execute him?"

"Go ahead and arrest him," I said, "but execution—no. That can come only after a proper trial."

Fate allowed Quang to get away. As the young officer and a friend were jumping into a jeep to drive the half mile to head-quarters, two Communist planes swept down and bombed the base heavily. The officers were unable to get out and Quang was never seen in Saigon again. I understand he is now living in Canada.

Bombing Begins at the Airfield

Those two planes signaled the start of a concentrated offensive on the airfield. The Communists knew that once the airfield fell, Saigon was doomed. The first heavy bomb fell three hundred yards from my house. By now nearly four hundred people were congregated there or in the grounds surrounding it—military families who had been hoping for seats on a plane, some deciding to sleep in the office or in nearby buildings at night. It was like a refugee camp. As the first bombs shook the house, one pilot ran into my living room crying,

"I am going to scramble."

I shouted, "I agree, go ahead!"

He rushed to the nearest fighter-bomber. I jumped into a jeep with a major and drove to the airstrip to see the extent of the damage. The base was uncanny, silent, deserted, in stark contrast to its normal busy life. Everyone had darted for shelter, and our jeep was the only moving object in sight. The Communist pilots must have spotted us, for the planes above wheeled around almost lazily, and then started strafing us. I could see the flashes of the guns aiming at the jeep as we jumped into a hole.

Scores of Vietnamese planes were destroyed on the ground. The electricity was cut off. We had no more communication with Joint General Staff headquarters and everyone in the house had to eat by candlelight.

About 9:30 P.M., the Communists started mortar and rocket fire, and by 11 P.M. I could stand the inaction no longer.

"Let's go up," I said to a couple of pilots and a navigator. We rushed out to my helicopter, took off and circled around. There were fires everywhere, the flames licking their way almost up to the perimeter of the base, and we could pick out the main Communist attacking positions easily because when they heard the noise of my helicopter they opened fire.

The biggest rocket battery seemed to be near the radio station.

It was impossible to scramble any planes on the bombed and pitted runways of the airfield, but from the air I managed to contact Can Tho air base in the Mekong Delta and they loaded up four planes with 750-pound bombs. There was no time for code names when the planes arrived. I just yelled into the radio, "This is Marshal Ky, find the rocket position, then go in and destroy it." As they moved into position, I watched from the helicopter, guiding them a little to the left, a little to the right, until they were dead on target. They destroyed the biggest bank of rockets. When I was short of gas, I managed to refuel at the Shell depot in Nha Be, outside the city. Dozens of planes were lining up for gas. By now everyone was waiting for the end. It was strange watching old friends—pilots and navigators who had fought with me for years. Most had lost contact with their commands, and looked to me for guidance. I told those whose ammo had run out to refuel and fly back to Can Tho. Those whose choppers were armed turned back to Saigon, to drop their last bomb and fire their last bullet on an enemy which by now had advanced to the fences of Tan Son Nhut, my air base. Then they, too, would head back for the delta.

I flew back to Air Force Command Headquarters at Tan Son Nhut. It was utter confusion. The entire air force command, consisting of about a hundred generals, colonels, and majors, were grouped in the commander's office. I noticed some army generals too. The air force commander told me the Americans had ordered all F5 aircraft to be evacuated to Thailand or the Philippines. The air force commanding staff were to wait in the office for instructions from the Americans who would evacuate them.

The Final Assault Strikes

Soon after dawn on the 29th the Communists started pounding the runway of the air base with their big Russian 130mm guns. Within minutes thick, oily smoke spread into a huge cloud as the enemy scored a direct hit on the main fuel depot. Several planes on the ground exploded in gigantic orange flashes, and there could be no doubt that the final offensive had opened. The Communists certainly knew that if they could destroy the air base there would be very little left of Saigon.

Evacuation and Desertion

Still I waited in my house, even when I began to hear the spatter of machine-gun bullets—and that sounded as though the enemy was in a cemetery about half a mile away. As I was debating what to do, a car drew up at the gate. To my astonishment the Stars and Stripes fluttered on its mast, and out stepped Ambassador Martin. At first I assumed he was coming to see me, but of course that could not be possible, for he had no idea where I was. I heard later that it had taken him two hours to make the journey from the embassy and he had driven to the airfield with General Homer Smith because he could not believe it was now impossible to land planes at the base—which meant that the Americans could no longer organize a large-scale evacuation, but would have to carry people out of Vietnam in helicopters, making it impossible for Martin to keep his promise that all Vietnamese connected with the embassy would be evacuated.

Martin stayed only a few minutes and I can imagine his despair after driving around the airfield in a jeep and seeing that it was unserviceable. Then he and General Smith climbed back into his car.

However desperate the situation, I still clung to some hope. Climbing into my chopper I headed for the Joint General Staff headquarters. Perhaps I could make contact with other units, and perhaps urge them to reorganize their ranks to fight. But at JGS, I was told that the chief of staff had resigned and left Vietnam two days previously. The compound, normally filled with thousands of officers and soldiers, was almost deserted. I went up to the office of the chief of staff, and found it occupied by Lieutenant General Don Van Khuyen, acting chief of staff. I tried in vain to contact the navy and other units. Poor General Khuyen! He was alone and helpless. At 11:30 A.M., looking out over Saigon, I could see Air America planes filling up the sky. That meant the evacuation of Americans and Vietnamese government officials had started.

This was the moment when I realized all hope had gone. I called the Air Force Command again. The staff had moved to the U.S. defense attaché office and were being evacuated. I decided to leave, too. As I walked down the stairs, I met General Truong, former commander of Military Region I. "What are you doing here?" I asked him. Truong replied, "I don't know what to do any more." His family had left several days previously, so I told him, "Come along with me, then." I collected a dozen or so flyers, and we all piled aboard my helicopter as I started the motors whirring. I had hardly time to glance back at my house, where so much had happened, where the youngsters had been laughing only the previous morning, before we were over the city looking down on the streets alive with scurrying figures, the orange flames of fires dotting the picture. It all passed quickly—my last sight of beloved Saigon—as we headed out toward the sea. Every size and shape of vessel, from puny rowboats to carriers, seemed to fill the blue waters. Switching my radio on to a rescue emergency frequency, I made crackling contact with the U.S. carrier *Midway*, lying just off the coast. Willing voices guided me down to the deck.

The commander of the *Midway* was an old friend, Admiral Harris, who years previously I had decorated for his bravery and help to Vietnam, and he came forward to greet me, shook hands, and started to ask, "How are you?" But then he saw my face and left the sentence unfinished. Try as I could, it was hard to hold back the tears; very touchingly the admiral left me alone for a quarter of an hour before flying me in a helicopter to the U.S. command ship, the *Blue Ridge*.

Just before I boarded the chopper, I realized I had one last thing to do. I went back to my own helicopter, unbuckled my revolver, and laid it on the pilot's seat. It suddenly occurred to me that as the guest of another country I might have to hand in my gun, and I had visions of the manner in which a defeated commander hands over the sword. The situation was not quite analogous, but nonetheless I wanted to avoid the symbolic gesture.

Suspicion of Evacuees

I hate to sound ungrateful, but the initial hospitality on the *Blue Ridge* was rather different from that on the *Midway*.

When fourteen of us—all high-ranking officers—stepped out of the helicopter, the first words of welcome by an officious American colonel were a shout, "All of you, come here." He directed us to a table and asked, "Have you any objections to being searched?" Halfway through this procedure somebody whispered to him. The colonel said to me in a low voice, "You, please come with me." He took me to his cabin and asked, "Where do you come from—Saigon?" I nodded. Finally he blurted out, "Are you Mr. Ky?" I nodded again. Later that night, after I had been to see the commanding officer, the colonel came to apologize, and I told him that I fully appreciated the confusion, even suspicion, everywhere. But I could not forbear to add, "I understand that you might be suspicious, but after all, we have *all* sacrificed everything in this war. We may have lost, but we are not the *only* losers—you Americans have lost, too. What I can't understand is—why did you have to treat the officers who were with me the way you did? After all, we have been comrades in arms. We are not Communists, you know."

CHRONOLOGY

1960
Richard Nixon and John F. Kennedy debate on television; African American students protest segregation by sitting at all-white lunch counters in Greensboro, North Carolina; the Federal Drug Administration approves the birth control pill; Willard V. Libby wins the Nobel Prize for developing radiocarbon dating; writer Albert Camus dies.

1961
Bay of Pigs invasion; United Nations condemns apartheid; Syria withdraws from the United Arab Republic; Amnesty International is founded; Berlin Wall is built; Uri Gagarin of the Soviet Union is first human to go to outer space in a rocket; writer Ernest Hemingway dies; Harper Lee wins the Pulitzer Prize for Fiction for *To Kill a Mockingbird*.

1962
Cuban Missile Crisis; Second Vatican Council begins meeting; computer developers begin work on a network that is the predecessor of the Internet; astronaut John Glenn of the United States orbits the earth; publication of Rachel Carson's *Silent Spring;* John Steinbeck wins the Nobel Prize for Literature; writer William Faulkner dies.

1963
John F. Kennedy is assassinated; Martin Luther King Jr. organizes the March on Washington supporting proposed civil rights legislation; Betty Friedan's *The Feminine Mystique* is published; Linus Pauling, an American chemist, wins the second unshared Nobel Prize (only winner with this distinction); Valentina Ter-shkova of the Soviet Union becomes the first woman in outer space; Beatles first number-one song in England, "Please Please Me"; poet Robert Frost, writers Flannery O'Connor and C.S. Lewis die.

1964

Gulf of Tonkin Resolution; Martin Luther King Jr. awarded the Nobel Peace Prize; Alexi Kosygin and Leonid Brezhnev replace Soviet premier Nikita Khrushchev; the Palestine Liberation Organization is founded; Jean-Paul Sartre wins (and declines) the Nobel Prize for Literature.

1965

Malcolm X is assassinated; Congress establishes Medicare; state troopers attack African American protesters in Selma, Alabama; war erupts between India and Pakistan; former British prime minister Winston Churchill dies; poet T. S. Eliot dies.

1966

The Cultural Revolution begins in China; The U.S. Congress passes the Freedom of Information Act making classified documents publicly accessible; the Soviets complete an unmanned moon landing; Huey Newton and Bobby Seale establish the Black Panther Party; National Organization for Women is founded.

1967

South African heart surgeon Christiaan Neethling Barnard performs the first human heart transplant; Israel emerges victorious from the Six-Day War; China tests its first hydrogen bomb; American scientist Dian Fossey sets up a permanent camp in Rwanda to research primates; race riots occur in Detroit, Michigan, and Newark, New Jersey.

1968

Martin Luther King Jr. is assassinated; protests at the democratic convention in Chicago lead to violence; senator and presidential hopeful Robert Kennedy is assassinated; the Tet Offensive occurs in Vietnam; My Lai massacre in Vietnam; American students and youth organize numerous protests against the war in Vietnam; *Apollo 8* orbits the moon with three American astronauts aboard; Pope Paul VI speaks out against artificial means of birth control; Queen Elizabeth II appoints new Poet Laureate C. Day Lewis; writer John Steinbeck dies.

1969

U.S. astronauts land on the Moon; New York City's Stonewall riot initiates the gay rights movement; Shirley Chisholm is sworn in as the first African American female member of Congress; music festival Woodstock occurs; Samuel Beckett wins the Nobel Prize for Literature.

1970

American military involvement in Vietnam is extended to Cambodia, resulting in major antiwar protests, including those at Kent State that result in four student protesters being killed by the National Guard; American biochemist Har Gobind Khorana produces the first artificial DNA; a typhoon hits East Pakistan and resulting floods kill five hundred thousand people.

1971

New diplomatic efforts bring about détente between America and China; three-dimensional imaging technology (the CAT scan) is developed in England; Jane Goodall's *In the Shadow of Man* is published.

1972

Watergate break-in; eleven Israeli athletes are killed by Arab terrorists in the Olympic village in Munich; East Pakistan becomes the independent nation of Bangladesh; Gloria Steinem founds *Ms.* magazine.

1973

The Arab oil embargo begins, resulting in oil crisis for United States, Japan, and Europe; Salvador Allende, Chile's political leader, is overthrown by a military coup; *Roe v. Wade* legalizes abortion in all fifty states; American space station and orbiting laboratory, Skylab, is launched; writer J.R.R. Tolkien dies.

1974

President Richard Nixon resigns; new president Gerald Ford pardons Nixon; Ethiopia's emperor, Haile Selassie, is overthrown; Portugal's military dictatorship is overthrown; Hank Aaron hits his 715th home run, breaking Babe Ruth's record.

1975

Saigon falls to Communist opposition, new Cambodian leader Pol Pot begins the genocide that ultimately claims 2 million lives; civil war between Muslims and Christians erupts in Lebanon; in Spain, King Juan Carlos ascends to power and begins democratic reforms; archaeologists in China discover six thousand life-sized pottery military figures.

1976

Chinese Communist leader Mao Zedong dies and is succeeded by Hua Guofeng; riots break out in Soweto, South Africa; the U.S. National Academy of Sciences announces that chlorofluorocarbons (CFCs) can be destructive to the ozone; publication of Alex Haley's *Roots.*

1977

Based on Haley's best-selling book *Roots*, the television miniseries attracts the largest audience in television history.

1978

Marxist Sandinista guerrillas overthrow the Nicaraguan government; Polish cardinal Karol Wojtyla becomes the first non-Italian pope in more than 450 years; birth of the first test-tube baby.

1979

The Ayatollah Khomeini deposes the shah of Iran; Margaret Thatcher becomes the first female prime minister of England; nuclear accident at Three Mile Island; a slight ring of debris around Jupiter is discovered by in-space telescope *Voyager I.*

FOR FURTHER RESEARCH

Jonathan Alter, "The Real Echoes from Vietnam," *Newsweek*, April 14, 2003.

Terry H. Anderson, *The Movement and the Sixties*. New York: Oxford University Press, 1996.

Matthew J. von Bencke, *The Politics of Space: A History of U.S.-Soviet/Russian Competition and Cooperation in Space*. Boulder, CO: Westview, 1997.

Kenneth J. Bindas, ed., *America's Musical Pulse: Popular Music in Twentieth-Century Society*. Westport, CT: Praeger, 1992.

Rachel Carson, *Silent Spring*. 1962. Reprint, Boston: Houghton Mifflin, 2002.

Barbara Hinkson Craig and David M. O'Brien, *Abortion and American Politics*. Chatham, NJ: Chatham House, 1993.

James DeFronzo, *Revolutions and Revolutionary Movements*. Boulder, CO: Westview, 1991.

Dwight D. Eisenhower, "Notes on Luncheon Meeting," April 22, 1961, Eisenhower Library, Papers, Post-Presidential, 1961–1969, Box 11: Kennedy, John F., 1962.

David Farber, *The Sixties: From Memory to History*. Chapel Hill: University of North Carolina Press, 1994.

Lawrence Freedman, *Kennedy's Wars: Berlin, Cuba, Laos, and Vietnam*. New York: Oxford University Press, 2000.

Paul Friedlander, *Rock and Roll: A Social History*. Boulder, CO: Westview, 1996.

Chana Gazit, producer, director, and writer, "The Pill," PBS *American Experience* series, February 24, 2003.

Jeff Guinn, "We Loved Them Yeah, Yeah, Yeah," *Fort Worth Star-Telegram*, February 8, 1994.

Maurice Halperin, *The Rise and Decline of Fidel Castro: An Essay in Contemporary History.* Berkeley and Los Angeles: University of California Press, 1972.

George Harrison et al., "1964," in *The Beatles Anthology.* San Francisco: Chronicle Books, 2000.

Betsy Hartmann, *Reproductive Rights and Wrongs: The Global Politics of Population Control.* Cambridge, MA: South End, 1995.

Jim F. Heath, *Decade of Disillusionment: The Kennedy-Johnson Years.* Bloomington: Indiana University Press, 1975.

Max Holland, "The Key to the Warren Report," *American Heritage*, November 1995.

Maurice Isserman and Michael Kazin, *America Divided: The Civil War of the 1960s.* New York: Oxford University Press, 2000.

Lyndon B. Johnson, "Address to Joint Session of the House and Senate," *Congressional Record*, 88th Cong., 1st sess., 109, part 17, November 27, 1963.

Michael Karwowski, "Fifty Years of British Popular Culture," *Contemporary Review*, November 2002.

Robert F. Kennedy, "On the Death of Martin Luther King Jr.," April 4, 1968, Indianapolis, *Senate Papers, Speeches, and Press Releases*, John F. Kennedy Library, Boston.

Roger Kimball, "What the Sixties Wrought," *New Criterion*, March 1999.

Michael J. Kryzanek, *U.S.–Latin American Relations.* Westport, CT: Praeger, 1996.

Nguyen Cao Ky, *Twenty Years and Twenty Days.* New York: Stein and Day, 1976.

Alan J. Levine, *The Missile and Space Race.* Westport, CT: Praeger, 1994.

Peter B. Levy, ed., *America in the Sixties—Right, Left, and Center: A Documentary History.* Westport, CT: Praeger, 1998.

Michael Lynch, "Mao Zedong: Liberator or Oppressor of China?" *History Review*, 2002.

Myron A. Marty, *Daily Life in the United States, 1960–1990: Decades of Discord.* Westport, CT: Greenwood, 1997.

Randall M. Miller, ed., *The 1960s Cultural Revolution.* Westport, CT: Greenwood, 2000.

Edward P. Morgan, *The 60s Experience: Hard Lessons About Modern America.* Philadelphia: Temple University Press, 1991.

Richard M. Nixon, April 30, 1973, speech broadcast live to American public.

Joseph M. Petulla, *American Environmentalism: Values, Tactics, Priorities.* College Station: Texas A&M University Press, 1980.

Stephen G. Rabe, "After the Missiles of October: John F. Kennedy and Cuba, November 1962 to November 1963," *Presidential Studies Quarterly*, December 2000.

James Reed, *From Private Vice to Public Virtue: The Birth Control Movement and American Society Since 1830.* New York: BasicBooks, 1978.

John Rodden, "The Berlin Wall Lives: Today, It's a Mental Construct," *Commonweal*, September 22, 2000.

Robert D. Schulzinger, *A Time for War: The United States and Vietnam, 1941–1975.* New York: Oxford University Press, 1997.

Gilbert Y. Steiner, ed., "The Conflict over Constitutional Legitimacy," in *The Abortion Dispute and the American System.* Washington, DC: Brookings Institute, 1983.

Howard Trivers, *Three Crises in American Foreign Affairs and a Continuing Revolution.* Carbondale: Southern Illinois University Press, 1972.

Colin Tudge, "The Great Green Book," *New Statesman*, April 19, 1999.

Wyn Wachhorst, *The Dream of Spaceflight.* New York: Basic Books, 2000.

Craig Waddell, ed., "Chemical Fallout: *Silent Spring*, Radioactive Fallout, and the Environmental Movement," in *And No Birds Sing: Rhetorical Analysis of Rachel Carson's Silent Spring*. Carbondale: Southern Illinois University Press, 2000.

David Wetzel, *From the Berlin Museum to the Berlin Wall: Essays on the Cultural and Political History of Modern Germany*. Westport, CT: Praeger, 1996.

Theodore H. White, *Breach of Faith: The Fall of Richard Nixon*. New York: Atheneum, 1975.

Thomas C. Wright, *Latin America in the Era of the Cuban Revolution*. Westport, CT: Praeger, 2001.

INDEX